OVER THE MOON

Palmetto Publishing Group
Charleston, SC

Over the Moon

First Edition
Copyright TXu2-167-182

Printed in the United States

ISBN-13: 978-1-64111-861-3
ISBN-10: 1-64111-861-X

OVER THE MOON

MY ADVENTURES DEALING WITH CULTS

Keith Musser

PREFACE

Before I get started, it is important I clarify that the names of these characters have been changed to protect them from harm, prosecution, or possible death. These stories are about events that either I experienced firsthand or were told to me about religious cults, mind control, brainwashing and deprogramming. These are things that operate in the shadows of our society that most people do not realize are happening. To help better understand what I am about to tell you, here are some general definitions:

Cult: a system in which venerates one particular individual, idea, or object.

Deprogramming: measures aimed at bringing a person that has been indoctrinated into a given belief system to recognize that he/ she has been indoctrinated. So as to gain his/her agreement to abandon allegiance to the religious, economic, or social group associated with the belief system.

Brainwashing: the attempt to change the thoughts and beliefs of another person against their will.

Bodyguard: a staff member trained to ensure the safety of all involved.

These stories are being written by me through the eyes of someone that has experienced firsthand events.

THE BEGINNING

Growing up in rural PA my family did not have much money. My parents lost their home because they could not afford the mortgage payments. Being from a less fortunate class, I was always daydreaming of being someone else. A spy or a superhero.

One day when I was in my early twenties, I was daydreaming as usual while watching television. I was abruptly snapped out of my daydream when I heard a voice I recognized coming from the television. I focused my attention on the voice I was hearing. On one of the local channels there was a friend of mine from school. He was speaking on the subjects of mind control and religious cults. I was shocked to say the least. I found out later they were supposed to dub his voice and hide his face for his own safety. As a result of that error, and recognizing his voice, I was drawn in. The words coming from his mouth were fascinating and just like that I was hooked. For those people who are not familiar with mind control or religious cults, you are not alone. I, like you, had never heard of such a thing.

Some of you may have seen some of these cult members soliciting flowers and trinkets on the streets and at the airports. Most of these young adults peddling these goods on the streets are from good wholesome upbringings. As my stories begin to unfold, I will unveil more about these seemingly harmless acts in further detail.

After hearing my old schoolmate talking about private investigators and stake outs, I knew that was the life I was going to live. It started my life down a road I had only dreamt about as a boy. I was about to become a real-life superhero. I contacted my friend and requested a position with his company. Needless to say, I was anxious, but eager to begin this new adventure. The following day I received a phone call asking me to help out on a case. They needed me right away. I could not believe it was happening so quickly. I was going to be the private eye I had only dreamed about. The emotions were overwhelming. I was nervous, scared, excited and thrilled. I was a ball of nervous energy. I was ready to start this new chapter in my life.

INTRODUCTION

Let me give you some insight into one of the cults we deal with. Reverend Sun Myung Moon started the cult known as the Unification Church in Korea. Then he expanded his church into the United States and several other countries. The cult took on the name the Moonies. Reverend Moon died at the age of ninety-two. But not before he became a very wealthy man. After this death, his daughter Jinn Moon took over his ministry and changed the name to Loving Life Ministries. Some people believe it was done to derail dozens of investigations into the Moonies. Moon bought up land and houses all over the United States where he set up shop. One of the cities he chose was San Francisco California where he bought a six-hundred-acre farm. This is where all his new recruits are sent for twenty-one days to be indoctrinated into the Moonies. Yes, you heard that right. After going through twenty- one days of brain washing, they are sent onto the streets to solicit Moons goods. Others become recruiters for the cult. I know exactly what you are thinking. I had never heard of such a thing in my life either, but it is real. Moon uses a slip at what is called Fishermen's Wharf, among other locations to recruit his new members. Fishermen's Wharf is located at a prime location where many visitors show up year-round. It is a beautiful place but very dangerous.

Once these kids see pictures of the farm and they are told about how they grow their own food, it is hard for them to resist. To a kid off the streets it is laughable, but to a naïve kid from the suburbs, it is the hook line and sinker. Once they have your interest you are invited to have dinner with them at their house. This is where it all begins. Everyone is treated with love and kindness. Once dinner is over there is a short film shown of the farm and everyone is invited to share in the experience on the farm. Very few people turn them down. There is a bus outside waiting to take everyone to the farm. What these young kids do not know it is a one-way trip.

Mind control is an immensely powerful tool and it is extremely dangerous.

Once these kids enter the farm, they come out of there members of Moons cult. These kids will work on the streets soliciting Moons goods from seven am to dark. They receive no pay and no medical attention. They are literally slaves to their so-called Messiah Reverend Moon. A good solicitor, of which Moon has ten of thousands, can make up to five hundred dollars a day soliciting.

These kids are brained washed in believing their families are evil. All of Moons members are required to denounce their families. And they do it willing. Moon drains all of his members of their worldly goods and they are told to drain their families' pockets as well. They do not hesitate to do so, as you will read in my stories. I believe I have painted a fairly good picture of what life is like for a Moonie member. As you read you will see the similarities of different religious cults groups that we have dealt with over the years. My job is to find these missing kids and secure them for our deprogramming teams. Once the deprogramming has been accomplish, they will spend time at our rehabilitation center where it helps them transition back to their normal lives. Yes, it is heavy, it was for me too. I had to learn something that was not taught in school. These stories are full of factual truths about religious cults. Some of these stories you will read may sound too strange to be true but believe me these things happen every day and have been happing for many years. Just keep an open mind and I will do my best to paint a clear picture. I hope you enjoy reading my stories.

CHAPTER ONE

MOONIE CULT: MIKEY

This story is about a young man I will call Mikey. Mikey got caught up in the cult known as the Moonies. Of all the religious cults I have been around the Moonies are by far the craziest. These cult kids earn money for the cult by soliciting flowers and trinkets on the streets. There is one thing that separates the Moonies from some of the other cult groups. The men are required to shave their heads but are told to leave a ponytail. They are brainwashed into believing these ponytails have a higher purpose. Without these ponytails they cannot be pulled up into heaven, and they would have to dwell on earth forever. Mikey was fortunate enough to have come from a wholesome family. He was a happy child growing up, who never wanted for anything.

All cult recruiters are taught to focus on financially well-off targets for substantial gain. Mikey was no exception and in a short amount of time the Moonies had recruited him. It was in San Francisco California at what is called Fisherman's Wharf, where Mikey said goodbye to his freedom and became a member of the Moonies. Fisherman's Wharf is a popular Moonie attraction site where they use a billboard showing their six-hundred-acre farm and how they grow their own food.

Mikey was sent to New York to solicit on the streets. Part of my job was to locate him. I learned of his general whereabouts from his parents and caught a flight out that afternoon. It was too late in the day for me to get started with my search, so I grabbed a motel room and waited until morning. These cult kids start soliciting early in the morning and do not stop until close to dark. I would need to be at their location before daylight. I was pretty familiar with this area because I had worked here before.

I knew the location of a couple of Moonie houses close by. I arrived early enough the next morning to see a van in the driveway. Shortly after daybreak, two of the cult members came out of the house and started loading their van. I needed to get a closer look at their faces. I left my car and walked down the street. There was no mistaking this was a Moonie house. All of the cult kids I was observing had shaved heads and a ponytail. I returned to my car just as they drove off. Mikey was not with them. By the number of cult kids that left in the van, I did not believe anyone was left behind. I would take this opportunity to remove their trash from the trash can in the hopes of finding out who lives in this house. I walked beside the house next door and around the back of the Moonie house. I grabbed their trash and threw it into the back of my car and headed back to my room. Once in my room I dumped the trash into the bathtub. The first thing I noticed was all of the paper products had been shredded. This eliminated any opportunity of learning who was living in that house. This also told me the Moonies had gotten smarter about covering their tracks.

I decided to wait until later to locate the other Moonie house. I did not want to be seen hanging around the next Moonie house with no one home. Just before dark I started on my way to the other house. The next house was located on a one-way street and sat farther back off the road. This was going to make it more difficult to keep a low profile. When I arrived, just as I thought, the driveway was empty, and the house was dark. Before getting out of my car I checked the neighbor's house and it was also dark. I did not want to get on the wrong side of the neighbors just in case I needed them later on. Not all cult members have good relationships with their neighbors. Especially the ones that are aware of what a cult group is. There is always the chance they would let me park in their driveway if it came down to it. Parking on a one-way street is not the wisest thing to do when someone is trying not to be noticed. I decided to take advantage of no one being home and grab the Moonies trash. I put the trash into the back of my car and decided not to wait to look at it. Just as I thought, the papers were all shredded. No help there. It was dark enough by now I was able to sit in my car and not be seen. All I needed to do now was wait. I did not have to wait long before their van drove by me. I knew I was not going to be able to see any of their faces, it was just too dark, but I had to give it a shot. They wasted no time unloading their van and going into their house. There was no sense hanging around now. I thought it better to return early the next morning.

I knew I was not going to be able to get close enough to see them load into the van. I decided to park around the corner next to a house under construction and wait for their van to drive by. Just about daylight they drove by me and I followed. All I needed to do now was wait and see who was going to get dropped off where. It did not take long for the driver to start dropping off the cult kids. It was not until the last group got dropped off, that I recognized Mikey. Boy did he look different without any hair. He was soliciting at a shopping center along with two other cult members. I had enough experience working with this cult to know what to expect. It was close to Thanksgiving and there were enough shoppers here for these cult kids to spend at least a week here soliciting. That is if the police did not arrest them for soliciting without a permit. They were going to be working this area for some time.

I had seen enough, and I knew what I needed to do next. I returned to my room and placed a call to Sara at the office to let her know I had located Mikey. I asked her to send in the rest of my crew and Mikey's parents. Whenever I was sent out to find someone the office had enough confidence in me to find that person. Sara had the rest of my crew on standby. Some of our security personnel lived on the east coast so it did not take long for them to arrive. As a company we were always looking for ways to keep our cost down and using our east coast team would help do that. This job was going to require between seven and ten people for this portion of the operation. That is a pretty big chunk of change in air fare alone. The average case could take around three weeks to complete. All of our cases are followed up by thirty days of rehabilitation at our rehab center. My whole team arrived the next day along with Mikey's parents. His parents were the first to arrive, so I took them with me to the last location where I saw Mikey. I had disguises for both of the parents so there was no chance of them being recognized. I needed them to make a positive identification of their son. I made sure we parked far enough away from Mikey to not be seen. Both parents had to take a second look at their son to make sure it was him. This was the first time they had seen their son in quite some time. To be seeing him like this was overwhelming. After we left the parking lot Mikey's mother told me it was all she could do to stop herself from getting out of the car and running up to her son and hugging him. I thanked her for telling me and for having the strength to resist. That would have been disastrous. It only goes to show we have to be ready for anything at any time. We went back to the motel where my crew was waiting for us. I explained to everyone what I had learned about Mikey's routine and what my plan was to remove Mikey from the group. They all agreed, and we set it up for the next day. Now all I needed was for Mikey to be where he had been the last two days. My gut told me he would be there. Doing this kind of work nothing is guaranteed. Part of my job was to inform the parents that there is always a chance for something to go wrong trying to remove their son from the group. The likelihood was that the cult would make sure we never get the chance to try again was possible. They would do everything in their power to make sure he would never be seen again. It has not happened yet, but you will read in a later story how our luck runs out.

The next day never comes soon enough. It is hard to sleep the night before knowing what we were about to do. No matter how many times we do it, it never changes. Putting all our thoughts behind us and focusing on the task at hand gets us through the things that need to be done. It was morning and it was time to make our move. Mikey had arrived along with his two other cult members and they had split up in different sections of the parking lot. This is where all the work I had done up to now pays off. We had everyone in place. The mother was with me in the pickup / getaway car and the father was in the backup car. Two of our security guys were already in the parking lot and it was time for us to do our thing. When the security guys were in place one of them would give me a signal and I would pull my car up next to Mikey. Then I would reach back and open the back door. One of the security guys would have already been standing in front of Mikey with a twenty-dollar bill in his hand, as if he wanted to buy something. That would get Mikey's attention. Our other security guy would come up from behind him and before everyone knew it, all three of them were in the back seat of my car and we were driving out of the parking lot. All of this took seven seconds. Our back up car would make sure that no one tried to interfere with what we had just done. We had less than an hour drive and we would be arriving at our safe house.

Our safe house is where the deprogrammers would be talking with Mikey over the next few weeks. Mikey had been pretty quiet during our drive, but things were about to change. Like most cult kids that have been taken away from their group, he was pretty angry, mostly at his parents for doing this to him.

He was about to show it. When we pulled into the driveway of our safe house, I explained to Mikey we were going into the house one way or another. It was up to him how he chose to do that. As soon as he got out of the car he tried to get away. He must have thought this was our first day on the job. The circle of security tightened around him and there was nowhere for him to go. At this point he was yelling at his mother and calling her all kinds of names. He was escorted into the house where he was taken to his bedroom. The deprogrammers were inside waiting for us to arrive. We had used this safe house before and had already made the house safe for Mikey's visit. The windows in his bathroom and his bedroom were screwed shut and the doorknobs were turned around so he could not lock himself in either room. The cult had taught him we were going to starve him and mistreat him. He was going to find out over the next few days this was not true. All he did for the first two days was chant. Once he figured out that was not going to get him anywhere, he stopped. He was also taught not to listen to anything we had to say, and he was doing a fairly good job of it. We were in no hurry so it did not matter how long he thought he could hold out. We were not going anywhere. What these cult kids do not know is that most of the deprogrammers in the US are ex- cult members. These deprogrammers do not say anything about their lives until the time is right. So, as far as Mikey was concerned, he was the only one in the house that knew anything about his so-called messiah. Boy was that about to change. Our security team takes shifts in watching Mikey twenty-four hours a day. Someone would be in his room or outside his room at all times and the door is always left open. Mikey's only thought at this time was finding a way of getting out of here. He would soon abandon that thought. Every day the deprogrammers would sit and talk to Mikey. Sometimes they would sit and read the bible out loud. Sooner or later he would start to lose the battle of blocking out what they were saying. The deprogrammers at one point will say something about the cult and he would start to argue with them. The more he argued, the more he was paying attention, the more the cult in him would lose the battle to fight them. He did not even know what was happening. These deprogrammers are really good. They know when to fight their battles and when to listen. It is definitely a skill with a lot of passion.

A week had gone by and he was eating well and was allowed to shower when he wanted. If he wanted something within reason, we always tried to help out. We would have his mother fix some of his favorite meals and he was enjoying sleeping in. He did not realize how much he missed this kind of life. Everything that he was doing was removing himself further from the group every day. Within two weeks the deprogrammers had done their job and Mikey had denounced his cult. He was now going through what all cult kids do when they have been successfully deprogrammed. He would find himself getting angry at himself instead of the cult for doing what they had done to him. The deprogrammers would stay with him as long as he needed them. After a couple more days I was asked to make travel arrangements to go to rehab. Both his parents went along with Mikey to our rehabilitation center. They would spend the next thirty days at our center, asking a lot of questions and getting a lot of answers. Mikey had been under Moons mind control and it was going to take some time before he would redirect his anger from himself to the Moonies. Mikey went back to doing what he was doing before he got caught up in the cult. All three of them are doing well. As far as the Moonies are concerned, they continued to do what they do and we continue to do our thing, which is to return these young adults back to their normal lives one at a time. As you read on into my other stories you will see some similarities in these different cult groups. I will do my best to keep these stories fresh.

CHAPTER TWO

HARE KRISHNA CULT: DOROTHY AND JAMIE

This story begins on a beautiful summer day in Ohio. I had just finished up with a case I was working on in Florida, when I got a call to head north. I was told to meet the parent of a young woman who I will call Dorothy. After flying in and grabbing a rental car, I headed for her motel. I sat and listened to Dorothy's mother who I will call Anna. Anna was telling me that her daughter had gone missing over a year ago, and she had not heard from her until two weeks ago. She said she had been shopping that day and when she got home there was a message on her answering machine from her daughter. The message said, "Hi this is Dorothy, and I am fine". She went on to say she had gotten married and his name was Jamie. Then she hung up. Anna had been crying when I arrived to meet with her, and now I know why. These were tears of joy. Up to now she did not know if Dorothy was dead or alive. Now she had a good sign that she must be ok. She had been crying because she was happy. Anna asked if I would help find her daughter and I said yes. At that time, I did not know if a religious cult was involved with her disappearance or not. All I knew, she was missing.

The police had done all they could up to this point. She was listed as a missing person. Anna was told by the police that her daughter had not gotten any traffic tickets, or she had not used her credit card. I asked Anna if we could go to her home, but I did not say why. I had a hunch. We had a six-hour drive to her home in Michigan. When we arrived, she told me she was separated since her daughter came up missing. I was glad no one else had been in the house. We walked into the house and I asked her to play back the message from her daughter. I was able to get some information off her answering machine that could lead to finding Dorothy. I retrieved the phone number where she had called from. Now it was the waiting game. In the morning I will place a call to a friend of mine and see if he can come up with a location of where this phone call came from. It was too late in the day to call his office now. Anna asked if I would like to spend the night and I said I would. The next day came early and I placed my call and asked my friend if he could run a phone number for me. He said he would, but it would take some time. He said he would get back to me when he found out. He did call back two hours later with an address assigned too that phone number. He said the number was assigned to the pay phone at the Cleveland airport. I thanked him then we hung up. I had just hung up from talking to my cousin and he told me he was just at the Cleveland airport picking up his sister. He said when he went into the airport, he saw what he called some of the funniest dressed young kids, and they were jumping up and down singing. He said they were selling a bunch of crap to anyone that would buy it. I asked him what kind of cloths they were wearing. He told me they were tied died sheets. This was definitely the Hare Krishna cult. The day he was at the airport was the same day Anna had received that phone call from her daughter. This would explain Dorothy's disappearance. Now I had something to go on. I have worked around this cult group before and that would help me in finding Dorothy.

The Hare Krishna cult movement in the sixties brought in millions of dollars for the cult. Each member is required to give the cult fifty percent of their income. But the cult teaches that money is evil. But not for them. What about this sex thing? This cult does not allow sex unless the couple is ready to procreate. When your babies are born the cult takes them away from you and that is the last time you will ever see them again. What is up with that?

Back to Dorothy. Anna gave me a picture of her daughter and she was a very good-looking young woman and I am sure she will be recruiting for the cult. My guess is she was with these kids at the airport. I asked Anna if she knew anything about Jamie and she said no. If I do find Dorothy, Jamie will be with her. This cult group does not separate married couples like other cults do. They will be working together. I asked Anna to stay home in case her daughter should call back, even though I knew she would not. I was surprised that she called her mother when she did. The cult does not allow their members to have any contact with their family members unless there is money to be gained. Anna did not come from a rich family so there was not any gain for her to call home. I was hoping I was reading this right. She did call home, which is not allowed, so why did she do so? I am hoping she might be having some doubts in her mind about the cult. That would be helpful. My plan was to leave the next day for the Cleveland airport. After arriving I decided to hang around the short-term parking lot and wait to see what turns up. It took about two hours before a van pulled in and out popped Dorothy and Jamie. I was guessing it was him, I had no pictures of him to go by. He put his arm around Dorothy, and she did not seem to mind. I snapped a picture of him for later. There were no doubts this was Dorothy. It was not going to be easy to remove both at the same time. But not impossible. I had made the decision right there and then we needed to grab both of them at the same time. I believed she would be harder to deprogram knowing that we separated her from her husband. I found out later how true that would be. We were not contracted by Jamie's parents to remove him from this cult. We knew nothing about him. All I did know was his first name and that he was married to Dorothy. Not much to go on. I knew enough about the actions of this cult group to know that they do not separate married couples. Jamie and Dorothy will be working side by side. I did not believe I would have the time to wait to see if they ever separate. I contacted Anna to let her know that I had located both of them and she was thrilled. Now I need to see if the two of them ever separate from the rest of the group. Somewhere close by had to be a house where everyone was staying. But where? I believed that both her and her husband would be soliciting and recruiting for their cult leaders. All I needed to do was find out where this was going to happen. Knowing what I knew about this group I had a good idea of where that might be. It should be taking me to the bad side of town.

This cult does not care where their new members came from. Druggies, alcoholics, bums it did not matter. Everyone was welcome. All they had to do was promise these types of people food and a place to stay. They are easy prey.

Dorothy and her teammates had been in the airports for some time now. I figured they would be here all-day. I went and found a motel close by and got some rest. After a couple hours sleep, I headed back to the airport. This time I parked a few rows back from their van. Just as I arrived, they were walking across the parking lot towards their van. I do not know how much money they took in today, but I am sure it was a bundle. It did not take long before we were heading out of the parking lot. I followed. We drove around for a while and just before dark they pulled into a parking spot in a rough area. What happened next surprised me. Dorothy and Jamie got out of the van and then the van drove off. Here they were with no transportation in the dark, in the middle of the spookiest place around. It did not take awfully long for both of them to walk into a bar. After sitting there for a while, I found where the police hung out just in case, I would need them later. After finding the closest and safest place to park, I sat and waited to see what was going to happen next. It was two hours on the dot when their van arrived back and parked in the same spot. One person got out of the van and went into the bar and within a few minutes five of them came out and got into their van and drove off. Yes, I said five. Dorothy, Jamie, their driver and two new possible members. After driving for a short time, they were pulling into their driveway. I had seen enough. I headed back to my room. It was already late, so I decided to call in the rest of my team in the morning. After doing so I called for my east coast team and then I drove up and got Anna. On my drive to Annas house I was thinking to myself Dorothy and Jamie had worked this area before and I figured they would do it again. I was counting on it. Once everyone was together, I would go over my plan to remove this married couple from this crazy cult. It would be up to my teammates to decide if what I was proposing would work. We started with one person to pick up and now I was proposing to do two at the same time. I had little doubt that they would not go along with my request, so I had already called for more security and deprogrammers. The next day a few of my teammates had arrived and I explained what I was proposing, and they all gave me the thumbs up. I was glad to see that. I was not worried about the other ones that had not arrived. They would never turn down anyone in need of help. Things should go smoothly knowing what we knew. Sometimes things happen so quickly we always must be prepared.

Our safe house had already been set up and all I needed was my two other security guys to get here. I got a call from them and since they lived local, they decided to drive instead of fly. They arrived a couple hours later. When they drove up, they were in a twenty-six-foot motor home. My prayers had been answered. Up until now I did not know how we were going to get both Dorothy and Jamie at the same time, but I knew now. I will fill you in a little later as this story unfolds. We were all set. All we need is for both of them to stay to their same routine and things should go well. Just like all our other cases the wait is always the hardest. We were ready for whatever happens. I had a plan. I needed to be at the pickup site to explain my plan in detail.

The next day came early and we headed for the pickup site. Once we arrived, I started going over my plan. The plan was to use the motor home as our staging area. It would be parked close to where the two of them would get dropped off. If my plan worked, it would solve the problem of getting both of them at the same time. The plan was to put five security guys on the street. One of them would approach the married couple then try to sell them some drugs. I knew they would not buy any, but it did not matter. Just as long as Dorothy thought she was going to be able to recruit this guy that is all I wanted. This guy was going to be me. One of the deprogrammers I had brought in was a woman. She would be sitting outside the motorhome in a chair posing as my wife. Now they would have two new recruits right in front of them. One for each of them. After asking them if they wanted to buy some drugs, I needed to lure them over to my wife. Once we had them next to the door, we had two choices. My wife would ask if anyone wanted any coffee. Remember both of them had worked twelve hours trying to sell their cults trinkets at the airport. I do believe coffee and the chance to sit down would appeal to them. I really believed it would work. If not, I still had the four security guys close by to help them into the motorhome. I was counting on my wife in playing a big part in getting them into the motor home. I told my wife when we got them close to the door, she was to say she was going in to get the coffee. I was counting on Dorothy to follow behind her. I would walk in behind her and hope Jamie would walk in behind me with my security team to follow.

Dorothy knows what her cult leaders expect from her and she will do whatever is needed to satisfy them. They had two new recruits right in front of them and they did not even have to work for it. By my calculations we had two hours to make this work one way or the other. It was about time for them to be showing up if they were coming. I believed they would. Just like clockwork they were driving towards us. Everyone was out of sight except for myself and my wife. They parked were they were last night and out jumped both of them. It did not take exceptionally long for their driver to drive off.

Ok now they are alone. I did not give them the chance to take two steps and I had already approached them. I had not gotten the chance to say a word and Dorothy started with her recruiting pitch. It was beautiful. I stopped her and told her I wanted my wife to hear this, and I headed towards the motor home. I did not even look back to see if they were behind me or not. I could feel their presence. We had reached the motor home and Dorothy wasted no time in starting her pitch again. My wife played it beautifully, she waited until Dorothy paused, and she said would anybody like coffee. I said I do, and she walked through the door. Just as I was hoping, Dorothy was right behind her. Jamie introduced himself to me then he commented on how good of shape the motor home was in. He said you must have paid a fortune for it. I said yes, but I got a good price because I paid cash for it. I thought that might seal the deal. By this time, my wife said the coffee was ready and I turned and walked through the door. It could not have worked any better because Jamie was right behind me. We had both of them where we wanted them. I asked them to sit down and they did without hesitation. One of my security guys had already jumped into the front seat and we were driving away from our parking spot. Just as we were pulling away the rest of my team jumped on board. Neither Dorothy nor Jamie had time to think about what just happened. I will never forget the look on their faces. To me it almost looked like the sign of relief. I gave them my normal speech. I told Dorothy that we were hired by her mother to pick her up and take her to a safe place where we had some people who wanted to talk with her. At that time Jamie asked did I talk with his parents. I told him no I did not. His response was then let him go. He did not ask that question with any heart and I took his question to have no merit. He was in love with his wife and if I were to stop the truck and open the door, I do not believe he would have left his wife. That was obvious. I explained to both of them the reason he was coming along with us was because we would never separate any husband and wife for any reason. I said we would never do that. When I turned to Dorothy, she had a tear running down her cheek. I knew this would be her reaction. One thing about the Hare Krishna cult is they do not believe in violence. They are more like hippies. I went on to tell them both they needed to stay calm and no one was going to hurt them. My wife asked if they would like their coffee. They both said yes. She handed them their coffee in Styrofoam cups, and I could tell they were enjoying it. At this time, I was convinced that this was meant to happen. I could sense the calmness that both of them were generating, but I was not going to let my guard down.

Both of them started chanting only stopping long enough to drink their coffee. It was quite funny. These cult members are required to chant over one thousand times a day to their beads. That is what makes it so funny. The rest of the trip they did stay calm. When we arrived at our safe house, they went inside without any trouble, but they did not stop chanting. For the most part they were doing what we had expected. The chanting would go on for another day until both got tired and stopped. Of course, we had them in separate rooms, and they were not allowed to see each other until the deprogramming team said so. I believe they both had enough of what kind of life the cult was giving them, and they were looking for a way out. They just did not have the strength between the both of them to fight through the mind control to do so. A couple days had gone by and both were showing some interest in what the deprogrammers were saying. Neither Dorothy nor Jamie knew the people that were sitting in front of them talking were ex cult members. One of the deprogrammers had been in the cult for five years and was high on the list of Bergs leaders. The other two were recruiters for the cult. We had a lot of experience with us and it would only be a matter of time before both would start asking a lot of questions. Dorothy came first. It took about ten days before she realized she had been under mind control and she was not leading her life on her own. Jamie was a little more stubborn. It took another week for him to realize that these deprogrammers had been through what he was going through. Then it was like a lightbulb just turned on. His skin color started to come back to normal and he was in a daze. Both were angry at themselves for what they allowed the cult to do to them. It would take some time for the deprogrammers to turn that anger away from them and to place it where it belonged. Back at David Berge. He was the one that took advantage of both of them and they needed to see it was not their fault.

I have always preached that mind control is an extremely dangerous tool and is extremely hard for any individual to overcome it by themselves. There is help out there. Our record for success thanks to the strength of these deprogrammers, we will keep on winning because we have the true God on our side. Whatever religion they may be.

The next week for both of them was the turning point. The deprogrammers had done their jobs and they decided to put both together and finish reaching out to them on any questions they still may have.

I did spend some time with both of them to see how they were progressing. These cult kids have never taken me as a deprogrammer nor should they. I have always projected myself as someone that cares for their futures and that seems to help in some small way. It is always the decision of the deprogrammers to make the correct decision when a kid has been deprogrammed or not.

Dorothy told me when I was alone with her in her room that she was pregnant. I asked her if Jamie knew and she said she was afraid to tell him. She always believed that Jamie would side with the cult in letting them take their child. The influence of the mind control put fear in her. She was afraid to lose her baby. The fear of not knowing what Jamie might do was too much for her to bear. I let the deprogrammers know of what she had just told me, and they went in to talk with her. By the time I left she was crying. I felt sad for her but again this was a good thing that was happening. I was in the room when she told her husband and the look on his face said it all. Now they were both crying. It was beautiful. Jamie was going to be a father without any cult interference and that made everyone happy. The love these two had for each other had never been stronger. And Anna realized she was going to be a grandmother and she started to cry. The deprogrammers just sat there and let them cry. Before long they all started hugging each other. The deprogrammers walked out of her room and besides the one security guy sitting in the doorway they were left alone to make plans on what was going to happen next. I was glad to see this for the hundredth time. It never gets old. The deprogrammers stayed with them for the next two days so I could get travel arrangements made to go to rehab. Before we left Dorothy told me that it was easy for her to change her mind about not hating me for what we had done to her. She said when I made the decision not to remove her from the cult without taking Jamie along showed her what kind of person I really was. The deprogrammers had to break through her mind control for her to honestly believe it. We arrived at our rehab center the next day and the deprogrammers would stay with them for the next month. That is the time it took for all of them to realize what had happened to them and to get rid of the anger they had and turn it into positive energy. I am glad to say they returned home and every one of them are doing great. The mother, Dorothy, Jamie, and their new baby girl.

I have said all along that we do not do this for the money. These extra security guys and deprogrammers came in here without any concern for their safety and stayed with these two young kids and received no compensation. This is not the first time they had done this, and it would not be the last. They did not hesitate to drop everything and come knowing the situation. They are the finest group of people I have ever been around. I am just a small part of what it takes to make things work. Put us all together and things get done.

CHAPTER THREE

MOONIE CULT: BRIAN AND LINDA

This story is about a religious cult called the Moonies. This young man that got caught up in the cult I am going to call Brian. Brian was your average young man, and when he was in eleventh grade his parents were transferred to San Francisco. He had the choice to stay with his aunt Dodie, and finish school in Ohio, or move to California with his parents. He was a good student and figured he would do well with the change. If things did not work out for him, he could always move back to his aunt Dodie`s home. Either way he had options. Brian had done well in sports and was into weightlifting. By his first year in high school he won first place in his weight class, and also played football and basketball. All of his activities kept him in tip top shape.

Brian was the first of the family members to move to California. His parents would be moving there at the end of the year. He wanted to get there before school started and take a look around. School had been in session for six months when he met a young woman, I am going to call Linda. It did not take long for them to fall in love. Brian went to one school and Linda went to another. They met by accident and of all places at a funeral home, where he had been working part time as a grounds keeper. Linda was at her grandfather's funeral when they met. It was love at first sight. They did not see each other for quite a while, only because he was a little shy. I know, a big strapping young man like that, shy. Go figure. Although he did not know how to get in touch with her, he thought about her all the time. One of Brian's classmates told him he was tired of seeing him moping around. His friend wanted to take him across town to a dance. Brian did not want to go but against his better judgement he agreed. When he walked into the dance club, low and behold there was Linda at the punch bowl. Needless to say, Brian could not get across the room fast enough. He did not even stop to pay to get into the dance. His friend had to pay the bill.

I know what you are thinking, where are you going with this story? I am going to tell you. Brian and Linda's life were going to change like they never thought possible. They danced all night and even after the music stopped. Brian wanted to give Linda a ride home, but she said she was going home with her girlfriends. After that both of them would spend every waking moment together they had. Going to different schools made it harder for them to spend time together. One Saturday Linda asks Brian to pick her up and take her to the park, because she had something, she wanted to talk to him about. So, he did. She told Brian she had met some genuinely nice people, and she wanted him to meet them. These new friends were people her father had met before he became a congressman. She told Brian she was invited to attend a free dinner with them, and she wanted him to go with her. Of course, Brian said yes. He was in love and he would follow her anywhere. She said she would set it up for the next Friday. They both decided to skip school that day and spend the whole day together. What he was not told was these nice people were Moonies! Linda did not even know them by that title. Her father had received donations from the Unification Church on a number of occasions. She only knew these people and what their image was from her father. Linda decided to go down to Fisherman's Wharf and let her new friends know both she and her boyfriend Brian would be coming to dinner next Friday. While Linda was at the Wharf the cult recruiter talked to her about their farm, and how they grew their own food. Linda fell in love with the whole idea. The recruiter told Linda he would like to know something about Brian. Linda loved talking about him, so she rambled on for quite some time. When she was done, the cult had more than enough information on both of them to use it to their advantage. What is that you ask, how could they do that? I am going to tell you.

Brian`s thing was weightlifting, and body building, and Linda's thing was all about conservation. I will explain how this all ties together shortly. Linda wanted Brian to experience this Fisherman's Wharf thing for himself. She decided to keep it a surprise until Friday. It was Friday morning and he picked her up down the street from her high school, and they headed for the park. They would spend the whole day there until it was time to leave for dinner. They drove to Fisherman's Wharf and parked his car. Linda introduce Brian to her new friends. He was led straight over to the billboard with the pictures of their farm. Brian was impressed. A few minutes later the bus arrived to pick everyone up for dinner. After Linda spilled her guts to the recruiter about both of them. The recruiter went into action and had everything ready for their visit at the house for dinner. I will finish this part in a minute.

It was dinner time and the cult bus pulled up and everyone got on board. After a short drive to their house, they were all herded off the bus and taken in the front door. Once inside they were told, not asked to remove their shoes. They were escorted upstairs and told to wait for dinner instructions. Minutes after arriving upstairs, Brian and Linda were separated. Brian was taken in one room and Linda to another. None of the other people were moved anywhere but for Linda and Brian. Linda's room was filled with poster boards with pictures and literature about conservation. It displayed a lot of phony pictures of so-called charities that did not exist. It went on to talk about the large sums of money the church had given to these false charities. To top it off, Linda was asked if she would be interested in taking the position of head of their operations in conservation. They told her she would be paid handsomely. They asked her if she would like to join them on the farm to further discuss this position. She was told if she took this position, she could share an apartment with Brian. She said she would have to talk it over with Brian, but as far as she was concerned, she would go. One down and one to go.

Brian was next. When Brian walked into the other room his jaw dropped. There in front of him were poster boards with pictures of everyone that had ever competed in weightlifting, and a lot of information on each individual's history. There was information there that was not made public, and Brian was seeing all of this firsthand. He could have stood there and read for hours. The cult leader went on to tell Brian they were in the process of putting together a security team that would be used to keep reverend Moon safe whenever he traveled around the world speaking to large groups of people. They ask if he would be interested in being in charge of such a large task. He was told whenever he would be needed to travel around the world, Linda could go with him. On top of that he would be paid handsomely. Brian was hooked. They told him they would like him to come to their farm to further discuss this, and he said yes. Just then they were called to dinner. When they walked out the door to attend dinner, Brian and Linda bumped into each other. They both were so excited they started talking at the same time. Until they realized, they both had the same dream. They were going to the farm together and as far as they knew they would live happily ever after. Boy were they in for a surprise. And so was everyone else who was going to get on the bus to the farm. After dinner all of them did get on the bus. What they did not know was it was a one-way ticket with no return. Every one of those kids that got loaded onto that bus did not know they would be staying on the farm for twenty-one days. This is how long it takes for the cult to achieve total mind control. Everyone except for Linda and Brian would be sent out on the street soliciting the cult's goods. All in the name of reverend Moon their so-called messiah. The cult would keep Linda and Brian at the farm for the rest of the year. Linda was kept busy working on meaningless conservation projects that the cult had no intentions of following through with. Brian was put in charge of security. The cult went as far as to have Brian and Linda pose in a picture with reverend Moon. It was told to both of them these pictures would be seen around the word. But in fact, they never made their way off the farm. The pictures were hung up for PR purposes. Both Linda and Brian felt honored to have met reverend Moon, but to have their picture taken with him, and have it shown around the world was overwhelming.

Both of them were hooked for life. The cult moved Brian's car on to the farm so no one could find it. He would later sign the title over to the cult. No one knew where Linda or Brian had disappeared to. Linda's father would have never guessed the Unification Church would be behind her disappearance. And Brian's parents had just arrived in California a few months earlier and had no clue of his whereabouts. The cult had done a good job up to this point keeping them hidden. Linda and Brian were separated for quite some time but were allowed to keep in touch by mail. Anytime the cult wanted to they would open up their mail and read it. If they did not like what they were reading they would throw it away. Reverend Moon rented an exceptionally large stadium and married thousands of Moonie couples, and Linda and Brian were chosen to be one of those couples. They were handpicked to marry each other. Even though they were very much in love, they were both too young to get married. They knew marriage was in their future, but neither one of them were ready yet, until Moon decided they were to marry. And marry they did. That is how it is done in the Moonies. What all the couples were about to find out was, right after they were married, they were all separated. Yes, all of the thousands of couples. These couples would not be allowed to see each other until moon decided it was time for them to procreate. Yes, I did say that.

When Brian's parents arrived in California only to find out that Brian had just left school without any reason. It was a year later his mother was put in contact with a parent group after contacting the police. Then she was put in contact with our office. After meeting with Brian's parents and listening to their story, we decided to take their case, and see what we could do. It was early summer, and Brian's mother had been contacted by an ex- cult member that had seen a poster with Brian's picture on it with the caption saying have you seen my son, and it had a phone number. The ex-cult member called the number and told Brian's parents, he did see Brian a few months ago. He said he saw him at the Moonie house, and he was working security. Now Brian's parents had hope. I had told his parents we were going to put a plan in motion that should flush him out into the open. We decided the plan we had come up with would do the job. The next day we put our plan into place. We collected some of the posters that were left over from the mother's earlier attempt to find her son.

One of our security guys went down to Fisherman's Wharf and approached one of the cult leaders. He asks if it would be ok to hang this poster on their board. The cult leader asks why. They went on to tell him they were hired by Brian's parents to find him. He went on to explain Brian's uncle had died and he had put Brian in his will. He also told him his uncle left him his farm, and they would not do the reading of the will until everyone was present. The cult leader looked at the picture and said he has never seen this young man before, but it was ok if he hung it there. Our security guy hung the poster up and few more of them on telephone poles and stop signs. The whole time the cult leader never took his eyes off of him. Now all we needed to do was wait. Brian had spent all his spare time as a boy on his uncle's farm. He had cattle, a bull and he raised thoroughbreds. He loved spending time there, and he was very fond of his uncle.

I met with Brian's parents, and I had filled them in on what we had done. I instructed her what to do if Brian were to call. I told her to act like a mother who has not seen her son in a long time. I also said it was ok to cry, which I knew she was going to do any way. I explained to her not to ask too many questions, just let him talk. I went on to say after Brian was done talking, ask him if he still wanted to go on that vacation that he was so excited to go on when they all moved to California. And she needed to ask him if he knew that his uncle had died. It did not take long before the Moonies had Brian call his mother. She called me right after he hung up with her.

She said he told her he had met a woman and they had gotten married. She asked him what her name was, and he said Linda. She asked if Linda would be coming with him when they came for the reading of the will and he said yes. She asked him if he could take the time to go on vacation with her and suggested that Linda could come along. He said he would have to get back with her on that. He asked when the reading of the will was and she said it would be Friday as long as he was going to be there, if not they would have to change the date. She went on to tell him they would not do the reading unless everyone was present. She told him he should show up Friday morning and she would know by then when the correct time would be. He said ok and he just hung up. She started to cry when he hung up, and she was crying when she called me. She told me he had just hung up on her before she could say she loved him. She said that is how they always ended their conversations. I told her his cult leader was listening to the whole conversation, and it probably was not even Brian that hung up the phone. It was his leader. That made her feel better. I knew it was Brian that hung the phone up and he did not feel bad about doing so. The cult had him believing she was not his family. I needed the mother to stay calm if we were going to pull this off. So, what we knew from that conversation between Brian and his mother was, he was going to show up sometime this Friday morning. We also knew the cult was not going to let him go on any vacation with anyone. Linda would not be with him when he showed up on Friday, but he would not be coming home alone. We knew we would have to deal with whoever came with him. I spent a couple of hours with his parents going over our plan when he would arrive on Friday. Both parents said they felt comfortable with what we had planned, but I was not so sure about the mother. It was Friday morning and we had been there all night getting ready in case he decided to show up early. We did not want his parents to spend too much time alone with their son. Not in the condition he was in under mind control, I knew his mother would blow a gasket, just like most mothers do. This is not the son they once knew. He was going to be bitter towards them without emotion. And that would be hard for any parent to have to deal with.

It was seven o'clock Friday morning and we were all ready, even the mother. Brian did show up at eight o'clock and he was not alone. It was not Linda. He had come home with his cult leader. Brian's cult leader had parked on the street just as I knew he would. They are taught to park where they cannot get blocked in and he did what he was taught. His parents were walking down the driveway, just as they were instructed to do. When they had reached Brian, he had already gotten out of his car. His mother walked up to him and hugged him, and he did not respond. She handled it very well, but I knew she was crying inside. The father tapped his son on the shoulder, and he walked back up the driveway and got into his car. He drove it down to the end of the driveway where Brian and his mother were standing, just like he was instructed to do. Brian told his mother the man in the car was going to come back and pick him up after the reading of the will. We knew better. Brian went on to say he could not take the time to go on vacation. He said he needed to get back right away after the reading. His mother asked back where, he did not respond. The mother was instructed to get into the front seat of the father's car and that is what she did. Brian did just what we wanted him to do and that was to get into the back of his father's car. They sat there for a few minutes. I had expected that to happen. We had put one of our hand-held radios under the front seat of the father's car so we could hear what was going on. The father knew what he was supposed to do, and we were in place waiting for them to arrive. Brian told his parents he had only enough time for the reading, and then he had to leave. His mother told him the reading was set up for ten am. His father said he was hungry, and he wanted breakfast before he did anything. Before Brian could say anything, his father drove off. He said they were going to go to a little breakfast place down the road. Brian did not say a word. I had told the parents not to get their son mad. I knew if they did, he would just get out of the car and walk away. Brian knew his leader would be right behind him ready to pick him up wherever they went.

As soon as the father drove off, so did Brian's cult leader, right behind them. Now it was time for our back up car to go to work. Their job was to take his cult leader out of the picture. In order to do this, they needed to get in-between his car and the father's car without being seen by Brian. His cult leader made it amazingly easy for our security team to do their job. The Moonies are not very smart about following anyone. We were in place waiting for the father to show up, but first we needed a signal from the backup car. It did not take exceptionally long before we got that signal. It said the perp was out of commission. We knew shortly after we heard that, the father would be driving by at any time. We were parked on the road with our hood up. Parked a couple of car lengths back from a traffic light. The father was instructed to pull around us and stop at the traffic light, and we would take it from there. The parents knew what was going to happen next and soon you will to. We were standing in front of our car leaning under the hood when the father drove around us. He stopped right where he was instructed to. The mother was instructed to keep her son facing forward by talking to him about Linda. The father's job was to make sure the doors were unlocked. Two security guys hopped into the back seat on either side of Brian.

At this time, the mother got out of the car and walked back to our car and got in. The father slid over to the passenger side and I entered into the front seat behind the wheel. After putting on my seat belt we drove away. Our back up car came by and picked up the mother and within a few minutes they were driving behind us. The security guy sitting on Brian's right side was six feet three inches tall and very well built. The one on the other side was an ex- college football player. Brian started to fight until he realized he was finally out matched. I explain to Brian he was going for a ride with us. When our ride was over, we wanted to sit and have a chat with him. I also went on to say, his uncle was in good health and he was looking forward to him coming back to his farm and spending time with him. I thought this would give him something to think about even for a short period of time. Hopefully, it would keep him calm. It must have worked; he did not say a thing the whole time we were on the road. He did not even yell at his father.

We arrived at our safe house and the security guys in the backup car along with the deprogrammers were standing outside of the door Brian would be getting out of. Brian for the first time in his life was surrounded by people that where larger than him, and he was outnumbered. It did not take much for him to realize this, and he got out of the car and walked into the house on his own. He was escorted to his bedroom and he sat down on the floor and started chanting. We were all expecting for him to do this. The deprogrammers went into his room with one security guy and made themselves comfortable. They were going to be there for some time. I went into the kitchen where both parents were. I could tell they felt a sense of relief knowing this part was behind them. It is a lot for anyone to go through. What we just did was illegal and dangerous, even for the parents. We were used to it, but they were not. I told them both I was proud of how they handled themselves. I thanked them for helping with what we all had done. I went on to explain to them Brian was really angry, and he was going to be for quite some time. I wanted them to know his anger could result in him getting violent with any of us, but especially his parents. And if he would act out, he would not have any remorse about doing so. I explained it was the mind control and not their son, I wanted them prepared. At some time, they are going to be needed to go into his room, but not until the time was right. The deprogrammers would decide on when. I went on to tell them there was going to be at least one security guy on the inside of his room and one on the other side at all times. We are trained to look for anger that builds up in these cult kids. Not all of them act out with violence.

Brian did what most cult kids do when they do not want to hear what someone is telling them, and that is to chant. Over time he would slowly lose that battle. Brian would spend the next two days chanting until he came to realize it was not doing him any good. He decided to do what most cult kids do and that was to shut up and say nothing hoping we would get tired and just leave. Boy was he in for a surprise. Like all cult kids they are taught we are going to torture and mistreat them. Brian was told he could sleep as long as he liked, and he could use the bathroom whenever he needed to. We went on to feed him like he had not eaten in years. His mother saw to that. We had secured the house before his arrival. After about a couple of days he saw there was no way out, so he stopped trying to get away. We had security on him twenty-four hours a day and he was not going anywhere. He tried to stay quiet for some time but that was not going to last long. These deprogrammers are incredibly good at what they do. They have the most patience I have ever witnessed. It would not be long before Brian would start to argue with the deprogrammers. Within two days he was starting to ask questions, and he was getting the correct answers to all of them. These two deprogrammers were both in the Moonie cult for years until they were removed by our group and deprogrammed. Brian was not going to get anything past these two deprogrammers, they are just too smart. Brian was a very bright young man and it did not take long for him to come to see the truth about the Moonie cause. Brian was successfully deprogrammed, and he went on to our rehabilitation center and is doing well. The last I had heard he was working on getting Linda out of the group with the help of our staff. Mind control is not only real, but it is an extremely dangerous tool, and it can and does cause physical, mental, and emotional problems.

CHAPTER FOUR

WAY INTERNATIONAL CULT: DOYLE

This story takes place in Seattle Washington. I had been working security at one of our rehabilitation facilities. Everyone that had the chance to work there loved it. This rehab center was a house just like any other house. The difference was it was filled with the nicest, kindness, kookiest people I have ever come to know. It had five staff members and at least three cult members that have been deprogrammed by our team... My job was to help any way I could. It usually meant taking these kids to the movies, the zoo, roller skating, playing racket ball, pool, pinball, and darts, or just taking them for walks. Well you get the picture. Having fun was my job. Being around these great kids, listening to their stories and being able to share my own is priceless.

Doing this kind of work is not something you can talk a lot about to just anyone. You might say it is a tad illegal. As I said in one of my earlier stories, working with this cult group is not on the top of my list as one of my favorite groups to work with.

I left my cushy job at rehab, hopped on a flight, and headed for Seattle. I was told we were looking for a little older fellow in his thirties. I met up with one of my other security guys that needed to leave for another case. He filled me in on what was going on. The young man we were looking for was Doyle. Doyle's position for the cult was going to take me places I was not looking forward to going. He oversaw making sure everything ran well for the cult when it came to drugs and prostitution. He was not someone you would want to get on the bad side of. The area that I would have to be looking for him could be dangerous. I checked into a motel after getting Doyle's file. Doyle had been known to throw his weight around from time to time. This was not going to be fun. I headed for the creepiest part of town. I knew I would end up here anyway, better in the daylight than after dark. After looking for him for two days, I stopped counting the number of prostitutes I bumped into. But no Doyle. I was not having any luck, so I decided to go on the night shift. This went on for a week and just about the time I was going to try something different, he walked out of the back room of a pool hall I was in. I could not take the chance of blowing my cover this soon, so I went outside and waited for him to leave. Unless he was sleeping in the back room, he should be coming out sooner or later. There were all kinds of strange people throughout the parking lot, cross dresser, people smoking pot and drinking whisky. I was going to blend in fine. He came out two hours later with a couple of his goons and hoped into his car and drove off. I followed. He drove for a while before he dropped off his goons and then drove off again. We drove for a while and somewhere

I had zigged where I should have zagged, I had lost him. I drove around for a while and it was not getting me anywhere. I drove back to the pool hall just in case he had returned. He did not.

After a couple hours sleep, I was back on the road driving around. It took me two days before I got lucky again. I had just finished my lunch at a pizza parlor. He pulled into the parking lot next door. Yep sometimes it happens that easy. That is why we call it luck. They all got out of his car and walked into an office building. It was four o'clock and the dinner crowd was just starting to arrive. The extra people in the parking lot helped me blend in better. Just a few minutes later he came out of the building got into his car and drove off. I decided not to follow him because I had a hunch he would be back. This might be the break I was hoping for. Wherever he had gone he returned in exactly one hour. As soon as he pulled into the parking lot his goons walked out of the building, got into his car and they drove off. I made the decision not to follow. I had been in too many sleaze bars and seen enough guns and knives to last me a lifetime.

I was betting that they were using this office building for illegal business, maybe money laundering. I was counting on them working out of this location for some time to come. I knew they would be back. After returning to my room I placed a call to the office and ask Sara to send in the team and his mother.

Going from day shift to night shift takes some getting used to. It was two o'clock when he pulled into the parking lot next to the pizza parlor. This is the timeline I was going to work off of.

I arrived the next day at one o'clock and got set up in the same place I was before. After going into the pizza place and getting lunch to go, I settled back and waited. It was two o'clock on the button when his car pulled in the parking lot. The same two guys were with him. They all got out and went into the building. I called the office to make sure my team was ready, and I was told they were already on their way. I was assured they would arrive by ten am the next day. I was grateful because it was already Thursday and I was not sure Doyle would be working on the weekend. I waited around to see if his routine was going to be the same as it has been. Just like clockwork he came out of the building alone got into his car and left. This time when he came out of the building, he was carrying a small bag. The kind of bag that you would get at a bank. This one was a little bigger and it had a zipper on it. He must have had it with him the day before, but I did not see it. The weather was calling for rain the day before and he must have had it stuck under his jacket. One hour later he was back, and his goons walked out of the building just like before. They got into his car and off they went. I had seen all I needed to see. They were going to use this office building again and again. I was sure of that.

All my team came in on time and Doyle's mother was with them. I went over the plan I had put together to pick up Doyle and everyone was on board. My team had already gone over what was going to happen with Doyle's mother, so she was somewhat informed when she arrived. She seemed to be calm. At least for now. We were going to pick up Doyle at the office building when he came out alone. That was better than to do it at the pool hall with all those crazy people and all the guns and knives. We were all set, and we were going to do this today in a couple of hours.

All I needed was for the mother to make a positive identification it is her son and we would make it happen. We all went into the pizza parlor just for luck. It worked before, why change things?

It was close to time and we were in position. All we needed was for him to come out of the building alone just like before and things should go smoothly. We were standing around in the parking lot and right on time, they pulled into the parking lot just like before. They all got out of the car and walked up to the front of the building. But they did not go in. They just stood there. We watched them look up and a few seconds later they took off running past their car and down the alley that ran behind the pizza parlor. Standing on the roof were five gentleman that looked like undercover agents. When they saw Doyle and his goons looking up, they tried to hide. The decision was made quickly by my team to get far away from here and regroup. After returning to the motel we all agreed these were federal agents that were on the roof and there were more of them on the inside of the building. They were waiting for Doyle to arrive. One of my teammates suggested that the agents were probably on the floor where Doyle and his gang should be showing up and that is why no one chased after them. That made sense. Whatever the Marshals wanted Doyle for was unclear. We all agreed they were there for Doyle and his gang, there was no doubt about that.

I told the mother I would keep everyone around for another day in case we were wrong. But I did not believe we were wrong. The mother agreed. The feds were there for her son, and they were a few minutes away from being busted. I went back to the parking lot a few hours later. I was not surprised to see four undercover agents staking out Doyle's car. His car had not been moved. It was sitting right where he had left it. I believe the feds had a bad bit of luck and they were desperate to make something happen. No one was going to return for his car. It was a close call for Doyle this time, but I knew it was not over yet. The feds were going to win out in the end. They had right on their side. I sent everyone home and by the request of the mother I stayed for two more days, even though I knew it was a waste of time. Doyle and his gang would not be showing their faces around here ever again. The cult would make sure of that. It was my belief the cult had already shipped him out of the country. This cult group has locations all over the globe. I told the mother if he ever gets in contact with her to call me and we would try again. I never got that call. One week later we were on to the next case.

CHAPTER FIVE

WAY INTERNATIONAL CULT: THERESA AND JUSTIN

This story is about two people that joined the same Religious cult. The name of this cult is Way International. It was founded by a man by the name of Victor Paul Wierville in 1942. The name of the group was changed to The Way International in 1957. Wierville claimed to talk to God, and God told him to learn to speak in tongues. His members payed millions of dollars to learn how to speak in tongues. Wierville went on to collect nine point seven million dollars cheating his members out of their worldly goods. He told his members the only way to get into heaven was to learn how to speak in tongues. Why didn't I think of that? Wierville believed the next world war would be a war between religions. He was preparing for war, so his members were taught how to shoot guns and how to handle explosives. They were also taught hand to hand combat. Whenever we took on a case from the Way International, we would check them for weapons.

This story is about two people that did not know each other before joining the group. The cult told them to get married. And get married they did. I am going to call them Theresa and Justin. Both of them gave up their worldly goods to learn to speak in tongues and they both felt it was a small price to pay to secure a place in Heaven. They believed in Wierville teachings, and to stay a member of his church they would continue to pay ten per cent of their income to him. This would go on for the rest of their lives unless we did something about it. This case takes us to Ohio. Justin's mother, who I will call Roberta, had contacted our company through one of the parent groups. A parent group is a group of parents whose children got caught up in a religious cult, and then were deprogrammed successfully. They band together to help fight against all religious cults. It has been their mission from the beginning to bring awareness to the public about the harm that is associated with mind control. These cults use mind control to trap their new members. Our company uses the parent groups to screen families that need help in getting their child out of these cults. We cannot be too careful when it comes to taking on any cult. The help these parent groups provide us is unbelievably valuable. There is no other way to get in contact with our group except through a parent group. My hat comes off to all these dedicated parents that give their time freely. After receiving a call from one of the parent groups I decided to meet with Roberta. After our meeting, I decided to try to help her any way I could. Dealing with this religious cult is not one of my most favorite groups to work with. When we take on one of these cases, we never know if it will be our last one. Wierville members are taught to do whatever is necessary to achieve his goals. Roberta told me her son got married to someone by the name of Theresa. She did not know anything about her, not even her last name. She went on to say Justin had joined the church a few years ago, and he has never been the same since. She was worried he might end up hurting someone or end up in jail. Roberta did not say why she thought her son would hurt someone. I did not pick up on what she said right away; it did not register because dealing with this cult anyone of their members can cause harm to anyone else. It is not uncommon. I could not begin to track down Theresa's parents, not knowing her last name, or where she came from. If Theresa is with Justin when we go after both. Roberta told me she had a cabin in Ohio, and we were welcome to stay there. I thanked her and I told her we may want to use it for something else. I asked her to call her son and asked him how he was doing and to ask him if he is still with Theresa and if he is eating well. Finally, she was to ask him if he needed any money.

I am using this approach to flush him out. I knew he would not turn down free money. I told her to tell Justin she was going to be at her cabin this weekend. If he needed any money to let her know, so she could take some money out of the bank. I told her to call me after speaking to him. She said she would call him right away. It took two days before she called me back. She asked her son if he was still with Theresa and he said yes. He went on to tell his mother that both of them would be at the cabin this Saturday morning. She told him she was really looking forward to meeting her daughter- in- law. She went on to ask him if one thousand dollars would be enough money and he said yes. They both said their good- byes and then they hung up. I got the address of the cabin and where the spare key was hidden. I told Roberta to show up Friday night and to bring enough clothes to last a week. I did not want her running late and not be there in time incase Justin would show up early. I was really looking forward to relaxing for a couple days before we got started with their deprogramming. We had a short drive to her cabin and when we walked in, I was in awe. This place was beautiful. I can see why people have cabins. Spending the next couple of days here will be enjoyable. The next two days flew by and it was Friday night and Roberta had just arrived. She showed us where we could park our cars. Her friend owned the cabin next door. She said they were out of the country, and they would not be back for another month. It is going to be helpful not having any neighbors. We sat down and went over our plan. Everyone was on board. It was Saturday morning and we were up early. Theresa and Justin showed up at nine o'clock, and Roberta was waiting for them at the front door. They entered through the front door and within a few seconds I walked in behind them. We had already turned the doorknobs around so no one could leave the house from the inside. I knew Justin was going to get mad and throw a fit. I did not want to waste any security personnel in watching the doors. By the time Justin had figured out what was going on, he wanted no part of it. He started for the front door and our security team stopped him. It did not take long for a fight to break out. Justin tried to throw a few punches, but our security team would soon have his arms pinned to his sides, and then they all fell to the floor.

We had moved all the tables and lamps anticipating this would happen. Theresa was standing right behind me and she started hitting me with her purse. Boy I should have seen that coming. After the stars went away, I turned around and took her purse away from her. I picked her up and carried her off to one of the bedrooms. I told her she needed to stay calm and no one would lay a hand on her. One of the deprogrammers walked into the bedroom, and I left Theresa with him. I needed to get back out into the living room where two of the security guys were dealing with Justin. When I got back, they had Justin under control, and he settled down a little bit. I told him he needed to stay calm and we were only here to talk with him. He said we had no right to keep him, and he wanted to see his wife. I told him no, not now. We escorted him into the other bedroom, and he sat down on the bed. The deprogrammer had already started talking to Theresa, and she seemed to have calmed down. Justin started using swears words directed towards his mother, and she was not even in the same room. I told Justin for a religious man he sure had a foul mouth. He told me to 'f 'off and then he shut up. One of the security guys had checked him for weapons and he did have a big knife. They took it away from him and we could tell he did not like it.

I went into the kitchen, got Roberta, and went into Theresa's room. I told Theresa that Justin's mother was going to check her for weapons. She responded she did not have any. I told her she was going to be checked anyway. She was telling the truth. I thanked her and we walked out of her room. I decided to rest for a little while; my shift was going to start soon. I tried to sleep, but my adrenaline was too high. I walked into Justin's room and shut the door. I sat my chair up against his bedroom door and I started reading my book. I would always keep one eye on Justin. There was one security guy on the other side of his bedroom door. One of the deprogrammers had been talking to Justin for some time now, and he was not paying any attention. At least he had not decided to hit anyone yet. That was going to change. It was late and the deprogrammer had decided to call it a night. Justin was just sitting there reading a book. A few minutes later he got up, put his book down on his bed, and walked over to me and got right in my face. I thought he was going to say something, he was that close. I just sat there holding my ground. I should have put my book down, but I did not. I had both hands on my book when he clobbered me in both ears. I jumped out of my chair pushing him to the ground. I got a hold of one arm, but he was too tall, I could not get my hands on his other arm. We both got to our feet. As security, we are not allowed to use force- Only restrain. All cults are taught that we will use all kinds of force to achieve our goals. This was one time I wished I could do more. It did not seem like he wanted to hurt me too bad because he hit me with his palms open. All I could hear was ringing. Justin was six foot four inches tall, but he was on the thin side. The problem was his reach was long.

When I had jumped out of my chair it made a loud noise when it hit the ground. Here comes the funny part. The security guy that was on the other side of the door walked in, and he was still half asleep. By this time Justin had calmed down and we had let go of each other. I thought he was going to go over and sit down on his bed, but he did not. He turned around and grabbed the half-asleep security guy and lifted him off the ground. His feet were dangling in midair. It was funny. He did not hold on to him exceptionally long. Justin was making a statement. The guy he was dangling in midair was one of the guys that wrestled with him when he first walked in the house. This was just pay back. He had no intention of hurting him. Justin walked over to his bed and sat down. He started reading his book just like nothing had ever happened. My four-hour shift was almost over, and Justin made no attempt to cause any more harm. It was time for me to try to rest but the ringing in my ears was making it exceedingly difficult. It took two days for the ringing to stop, and for me to get my balance back. I finally got to sleep, and when I woke up, I went in to check on Theresa. She was sleeping.

One week went by and the deprogrammer had not made any progress. I decided to go in and have a chat with Roberta. I wanted to get her up to speed on what our progress was. I told her about the scuffle I had with her son a few days ago. She got quiet. This was not normal. She did not ask if I was ok, or if her son got hurt. She said nothing. Something was not right. She was not telling me something, but what? The deprogrammer that was working with Justin decided to take a break. I decided to have a chat with him. I asked him what he thought about Justin's progress. What he told me confirmed my thoughts. He knew something was not right, but he could not put his finger on it. I told him about my conversation with Roberta, and we both agreed something was wrong, and the finger was pointing to Justin mother. She was hiding something. The deprogrammer decided to give it a few more days, and if he did not see any progress with Justin, both of us would have a conversation with his mother. It was time for my shift.

Justin was not talking to anyone, and this was not normal. We had been with him for some time now and nothing. Something was not right. I decided to try to get a rise out of him, a smile, or an angry look, something. I walked into his room and I sat down on the bed next to him. He turned around to see who was sitting there and why. He said nothing. I told him how he acted towards me a few days ago was not going to happen again and if he was going to pull a stunt like that again, for him to do it right now. I explained to him I had a book to finish and I did not want him interrupting me. His facial expression never changed, and he said nothing. I sat there a while longer to see if he was going to change his mind, but he did not. I took my position in my chair and I did finish my book. He just sat there quiet during my whole shift. I got with the deprogrammer and we went and had a conversation with his mother. She would not answer any of our questions. A few minutes later she started to cry. Then she started to apologize to both of us for not being honest with us. I thought to myself, now what. She let the cat out of the bag and told us everything. Theresa and Justin had been kicked out of the cult awhile back. She explained Justin had too many mental issues and the cult did not want him. She went on to say she had gotten him some help a couple of times. The last time he had gotten violent. Roberta said she was out of options, so she decided to lie to everyone to get some help. She went on to say the last doctor that tried to help Justin, got his nose broken. I was glad I talked to the deprogrammer when I did. Who knows what could have happen over the next couple of weeks if I would not have said anything? I called Sara at the office and I explained our situation. She agreed Justin needed more help than we could give him. My boss, who I will call C, knows just about everyone, and he had someone that could help Justin. C said he needed a couple of days to put it all together. I knew what needed to be done from here. I got the phone number of the local sheriff's office and I gave it to C. C contacted the sheriff and filled him in on our situation. He requested they send a couple of deputies to our location and pick up Justin and take him to the hospital. He went on to explain Justin was a danger to himself and his mother. The sheriff said he would help but he needed Justin's mother to call and make that request. C told him he would receive that call the next day. I decided not to tell Roberta until the next day. I was not ready to deal with her response. But I did inform my team.

The next morning, I sat down with Justin's mother and two deprogrammers. I proceeded to tell her what we were going to do. I explained she did not have a say in this. We were going to do one of two things, but we were moving forward. I told her she had no right lying to us, knowing his violent temper. I went on to say we were incredibly lucky someone did not get hurt, because when Justin arrived, he did have a knife in his jacket pocket, and given the chance he would have used it. She had put all our lives in danger, and we were not happy about it. I told her we had the proper help available for Justin. I explained everything had been arranged, and we were ready to move forward. I gave her the phone number of the sheriff office. She needed to call them and ask them to come to our location and pick up Justin. She was to tell them she wanted him committed to the hospital. She said she would not have her son committed to any hospital. I stopped her in her tracks and told her she had no choice. We were offering her the proper help for Justin and she was going to take it. She was shocked. But it did not matter. I went on to explain to her what our office wanted us to do, if she refused, and that was to pack up and leave. She would be here to deal with her son alone. I told her it was against my better judgment to leave her alone, but we would no longer going to put our staff in danger, to do something that could not be done. I picked up the phone and handed it to her, and she was shaking so bad I had to dial the number. She did what she was told. After talking to the sheriff, she handed the phone to me. The sheriff told me he would have someone to my location in a couple of hours. I thanked him and hung up. Roberta started to cry, and I got up and walked out of the room.

Our office was offering the help Justin needed and the mother needed to put her feelings aside and think only about her son. If she would have been truthful from the beginning, none of this would have happened. Our office would have gotten Justin the help he needed without the mother needing to hire us. I realize as parents we make some wrong decisions from time to time but lying never solves anything. I went into Theresa's room to see how she was doing. I sat down on the edge of her bed and asked her if she was being treated ok. She responded with yes, but she did not want to be here. Two hours later the sheriff showed up with one other officer. We had the coffee ready and they sat down. I told the mother to only answer the officer's questions and to say no more. Right before the sheriff arrived Theresa had decided to take a shower. The sheriff asked where Justin was, and I told him. I got up and led them to his room. He was sitting on his bed reading his book. I explained to Justin what was going to happen, and he said nothing. By this time, the sheriffs were standing over him. They told him to stand up, and he did not move. They wasted no time standing him up, and they escorted him to the back of their car. We watched them drive away. I went into Theresa's room and waited for her to come out of the bathroom. When she walked into her room, I told her what we had done and what our plan was for her. I told her Justin was no longer here in the house, and that he was on his way to the hospital to get some psychiatric help he needed. She did not believe me, so I walked her through the house so she could see for herself. She sat down on the couch and said nothing. I told her we were going to give her enough money to start her life over again, and we would take her wherever she would like to go. She sat there for some time. She stood up and said she was ready to go, but first she wanted to tell me something. She went on to thank me for being so gentle towards her when I picked her up and carried her into her bedroom. She told me she was pregnant. I told her Justin's mother would be so pleased to hear she was going to be a grandmother. She asked me to not say anything to her; she did not want her to know. I asked her if Justin knew, and she did not respond. I knew at that time it was not Justin's baby. She asked to be taken to the bus station. We all loaded into the car and I dropped her off on our way home. Justin was getting the help he needed. The last thing I had heard Theresa did not try to return to the cult. I believe she had learned enough at her deprograming, she did not want any more to do with the group, and I was glad. And yes, we did give her enough money to get started again. All our staff chipped in. I got Roberta to help as well.

CHAPTER SIX

MOONIE CULT: GERRI

This story takes me North to New York City. I received a call from a mother I will call Mrs. Parker. She asked if I could meet her and her husband in New York City. I flew out the next day and met with them at their home. They are like most of the parents of cult kids I have met, they were pretty frazzled. They had just found out their daughter was missing from college. I asked the Parkers to tell me everything they knew. Mrs. Parker told me they dropped their daughter off at college, and everything was fine. She said her daughter would call home at least once a week, and then the calls just stopped. At first, she said she was not that concerned, she figured her daughter who I am going to call Gerri had gotten busy with her schoolwork, and she would call when she had the chance. Then she got a call from Gerri's roommate who I will call Anita. Anita told her that Gerri had met some strange people on campus, and they were a traveling group. Anita went to her classes the next day, and when she returned to her dorm later that day, she noticed that some of Gerri's cloths were gone. She went on to say all of Gerri's schoolbooks were right where she had left them. Anita got concerned the next day when Gerri did not return to the dorm, so she called Gerri's parents to let them know.

I told the Parkers I had heard this story too many times before. Then I excused myself from them. I explained I needed to do some checking around, and I would get back with them. I checked into my room and I made a couple of phone calls. The first call I made was to information. I got the phone number of the college Gerri was attending. After being transferred to the dean's office, his secretary told me he was out, but he would return my phone call as soon as he returned. Up to this point I did not even know if Gerri had gotten tied up in any cult. As far as I knew she was just another missing person, but that thought was about to change. The dean of the college was the first to return my phone call. I asked him if he had any religious cults hanging around his campus in the last couple weeks. He said yes there was one group, and they were going by the name of the Unification Church. He told me he had the campus police run them off. I explained to him I was hired by Gerri's parents to find her, and it was my belief she had gotten caught up in the Moonies. I told him he would receive a call from Mr. Parker in the morning. I thanked him then I hung up. It was close to four o'clock before my office called me back. Sara gave me two addresses of known Moonie houses. Both were a few hours away.

I placed a call to the Parkers and told them what I believed happen to their daughter. I instructed Mr. Parker to call the dean's office the next morning and plan to get Gerri's belongings. He said he would. They could not understand how their daughter could get caught up in this type of group. I told them that was not important at this point in time. The important thing was to locate her and remove her from the group. They agreed. I explained to them I would do my best to make this happen, but it was going to take some time. I suggested they return home and wait to see if she called. I knew the cult was not going to allow her to call home; I just wanted them to get back to their normal lives as best they could. There was not anything they could do, and it would help to keep them busy. I explained I would call them as soon as I had something concrete to report.

One of the things I found out later was Gerri did not want to go to college; she was doing it because she thought her parents wanted her to. That made her easy pray for the cult. From what I could tell, Gerri's parents did not have any money problems. The cult recruiters are trained to look for high profile targets. I was hoping the cult had not gotten wind of her parent's wealth, at least not yet. If and when they did find out they would put her into hiding. That is the last thing I want to see happen. If the cult would find out she would be told to drain as much money as she could from her parents. Up to now she had not made that phone call home, and that is a good sign. She had been missing long enough to have been subject to mind control, and she would be on the streets soliciting. I was sure of that. Now all I had to do was find her. I decided to take a nap before I started my search. My nap lasted until the next day. After having a quick breakfast, I headed for the closest address

I had. There was a lot more traffic than I had expected, and it was a few minutes before dark when I arrived. I parked up the street and sat and waited. There were two vans parked in the driveway. I was not here early enough due to the traffic to see them arrive. A few minutes later the lights in the house went out. There was not any reason to hang around. I did not believe they would be going anywhere tonight. After checking into a motel and going over my plan in my head, I sat around for a couple of hours until I could not sit any longer. I decided to take a drive back to the Moonie house and see if anything had changed. Everything was just the same as when I was here a few hours earlier. I took a break from work and took in a late movie. After a good night sleep, I was back at the Moonie house early. The house was dark when I arrived but not for long. A few minutes later a couple of cult kids came out of the house and started loading their van. There was no doubt this was a Moonie house. After the van was loaded, ten cult kids came out and jumped into the van, and then they drove off. None of them were girls. There was not any reason to follow them. I waited a little while longer to make sure the neighbors had gone to work. I walked up the Moonies driveway and opened up the trash can. It was empty. No luck there. I had checked out of my motel room and I was ready to head to the second address I had. When I arrived it was too early for anyone to be home. There were not any vehicles in the driveway, just as I had figured. These cult kids were not going to be back until late, so there was no reason to hang around. After checking into a motel and trying to rest, I decided to return to the house. It was almost dark, so I did what I always do, and that was to park up the street from their house. I knew I was not going to be able to see their faces when they drove up, but I should be able to see the difference between male and female. It was dark when their van pulled in. When they got out of their van the porch light came on. Yes, there were girls and boys. I thought I had recognized Gerri, but I was not sure. I had seen all I was going to see for the night, so I headed back to my room.

I kept thinking in the back of my mind about what Anita had said. She said Gerri had met some funny looking people that were a traveling group. I did not pick up on that statement until now. What did she mean a traveling group? Where did she hear that? I would have Mrs. Parker call and ask Anita that question. If this meant what I thought it meant, I would need to go shopping for supplies I was going to need. The phrase traveling group is used by the parent groups to explain a group of cult kids that go mobile fund raising. If she is with this group, we could end up in a different state at any time. When these groups go mobile fund raising, they can be on the road for weeks. I need to be prepared. Thank goodness for all night stores. After stocking up on lunches, dinners, toilet paper, water, and a hose, I went back to my room and collected my thoughts. I tried to sleep but I had a hard time doing so. The cult group would not have told Anita anything about their work, especially about their traveling group. Where did she hear this and why? The weather had been changing and pretty fast. It had been cold for over a month. Mrs. Parker tried to reach Anita, but she was away on break from college. I was not able to find out what I wanted to know. It would make the difference of what kind of work Gerri was doing for the cult. Usually when a group goes mobile fund raising, I would take along one guy with me in my search. If she were soliciting from one location, I would not need any help. This cult group does not have a problem going mobile fund raising in the winter. They would work the ski lodges and inside malls. If she is mobile fund raising, it could take weeks to pin her location down for the pickup. I need her to stay put in one location for more than one day at a time. I had a funny feeling I was going to find out all I needed to know tomorrow.

I was glad I had gotten at least a little bit of sleep over the last few days because I was not going to sleep tonight. The next day came way too early, but I was at their house before daybreak. Now all I can do is wait. I did find myself falling asleep a few times, but I knew when the time was right my adrenalin would keep me awake. OK full tank of gas, warm gloves, hat, boots, and warm socks. Plenty of food and water. It was daybreak. Right on time the lights in the house came on, and shortly they should be loading their van. It took them longer to load their van this time. A lot more stuff and the same amount of people. They had so much stuff they had to pack and unpack to get it all in the van. They were preparing for winter camping. Yes, I did say winter camping. No motels for this cult group. I was so glad that I had read it right and prepared for this. I was not looking forward to this, but it had to be done. It was going to be tuff doing this by myself. Staying awake for long hours. Keeping one eye on them and one eye on the road and trying to read the map is too much for one person. Well it was too late to bring in some help now. They are pulling out of their driveway. They would have at least two drivers so if they are planning a long trip, they do not need to stop to rest. I am hoping they were going to pick one location and stay there for at least a week. Gerri is in the van I am following and that is the reason I am here. We had been driving for some time now and I had no idea what was going to happen next. I could not afford to follow them too close if I were going to be following them for at least a week or longer. I could not take the chance of being seen. I had almost lost them a couple of times. I know what it is like to lose someone you are following. It is a nasty feeling of failure. There is nothing worse than making that phone call to a parent to inform them you have to start all over again because you lost their child. I was hoping they would decide to stop and stay at one of the other Moonies houses available instead of camping. If there were any houses on our way. Unless they were transporting the camping gear to one of the other cult houses, I was sure camping was in their plans. The Moonie cult will camp anywhere. The campgrounds do not even have to be open in order for them to pull in and camp. No showers, no running water, it does not matter. It is cold enough for the ski lodges to be making snow, but they are not open yet. If they were going to camp it should be close to a mall somewhere. It is too hard to read the map and drive. I cannot see if we were close to a campground or not.

They had not stopped since we got started, and I was getting tired. I was praying they do not switch drivers. That would not be good. If I were to lose them now, it would be hard to find them again. It would be back to square one. They had driven too far, and it was too late for them to do any soliciting today. What was going on in the back of my mind were two things. I was going back to the fact that Gerri's parents had money. It was only a matter of time before the cult would find out. If they did find out it will change everything. The second thing is, I had lost kids before, and I do not ever want that to happen ever again. There is a lot of pressure in this kind of work and doing anything less than a top-notch job is un- acceptable. It is getting late and I have been tired for some time now. All I want to do is to lie in a bed for ten hours. Unfortunately, the Moonies had something else in store for me. Yep we were pulling into a campground. I did not dare follow them into the grounds. They could be parked around any corner, and I could not take the chance of being seen. I needed a place to hide and wait until they decided on what they were going to do next. That could be in one hour or it could be the next day. There is no way of knowing until it happens. If we were close to a mall they would not be leaving until around nine o'clock in the morning. But if it were a greater distance, that would be a different story. I located a maintenance shed that would keep me hidden from their view. They could drive right by me and never know I am here. My day was not over yet. As bad as I wanted it to be. If I was going to be able to sleep, I need to know if they had pitched their tent or not. Yes, I said tent. These nuts are in it for the long haul. There was too many of them to sleep in their van. By this time, the temperature had fallen, and the wind was starting to blow. I got out of my warm car and hiked down the path they took. As I peeked around the first corner, there they were parked. The state had put railroad ties across the road, so they were not going any farther. It was far enough for them to set up camp. I was happy to see this. I felt they were going to spend the night or even longer. All I could do now is wait. Now I can get some sleep at least for a while. I returned to my warm car and passed out.

I had no intention of getting up early but for some reason I woke up at five am, and I could not get back to sleep. It had snowed last night just enough to lay down a nice layer on the path we made coming into the park. There were not any tire tracks in the snow, so I knew they were still here. A couple hours later they drove right by me. It almost caught me off guard. Yes, I was half asleep. I could not see who was in the van, so I knew I had to follow them. We drove for a few hours and that told me they had picked up stakes and we would be spending the night somewhere else tonight. It was getting a lot colder now. I was daydreaming of a motel room when they pulled onto the exit. A few minutes later we were pulling into another campground. This one was not blocked off, so they were able to drive as far as they wanted. I could not see any place to hide so I had to follow them. We drove in for a short distance and they stopped and wasted no time in starting to set up camp. I was able to work my way around them by driving across the lawns. Now I was parked farther into the park than they were. I was not worried about them going past me and I was close enough to them to overhear some things they were saying. They were having a tuff time getting their tent up because the wind was blowing a lot stronger now. After they accomplished that, they started chanting, and it went on for some time. I got settled in for the night and shortly after that, the chanting stopped. Then their van pulled out. As far as I could tell there were only a couple kids that got into the van before it left. Gerri was not one of them. I decided not to follow. The rest of the group staying behind was not going to leave their tent tonight, it was just too cold. I could see the glow of their heaters through their tent. I did not even have time to lie down and their van pulled back in.

I was hoping they did not see the second set of tracks I made when we pulled into the park. Time would tell. No one seemed too concerned because they were not packing up, and no one was out walking around. They could have followed my tracks but to tell you the truth they were not that smart. So far, I had not given them any reason to think they were being followed. I slept through the night thanks to that piece of hose I remembered to buy with my supplies. I had learned my lesson from a trip before. I attached one end of the hose to my exhaust pipe, and I stretched the other end away from my car. That allowed me to sleep through the night. Waking up every couple of hours starting my car, so it would warm me up, you do not really sleep at all. This way I did not have to worry about the exhaust fumes, and the car ran all night. It was cold outside when we went to sleep, but it was a lot colder when we woke up. I was awakened up by the sound of their van starting. They had been up for some time and had already started packing up. As soon as their van windows cleared, we were on our way, but where? I was hoping for a Moonie house or an inside mall. It was six hours before we arrived at a larger town. We had traveled too far and passed up too many prime soliciting locations for them to waste this much time traveling across the state without a reason. I just did not get it. They made no attempts to pull in any cash to keep their leaders happy. Something was going on and I was not sure what to expect next. We were driving around in this town, and I knew something was not right. What we were doing just was not making any sense. Well I was about to find out. A few minutes later we were pulling into a Moonie house. What they did next gave away some valuable information, and I was glad they did. They were unpacking their camping gear, and putting it into the garage, all of it. This was going to be home for them or a place to stay at least for the night. That made me happy.

It had been some time since I had started following them and I needed to find a way of ending this adventure. It was mid-day and I did not believe they were going anywhere, at least for a few hours or even until the next day. I happily checked into a motel close to their house, and after two hot showers, and some good food, I kicked back and relaxed for a while. That was not going to last, I needed to be back at this new house before dark. Anything they were going to do from here on out was fine with me as long as those tents did not come out of that garage. It is time to get back to work so I headed back to their house. When I arrived, no one was stirring. The lights were still on in the house but not for long. They must have just finished with dinner because someone came out of the house and disposed of their trash. There were two vans in the driveway when I was here last and neither one had been moved. I believed they were in for the night. I stayed until the lights went out and then I headed for my warm bed.

I had no trouble falling asleep. I woke up early and I was back at their house. It was still too early, so I parked up the street. I would wait until people started stirring before I would move in closer. It was over one hour before someone came out of the house and got both vans started. I moved in closer. Shortly after that everyone came out of the house got into the vans and they drove off. Gerri was not with them. What was going on? I was not sure. Was she still in the house or did she get picked up during the night, and if so why? Boy I did not have a clue. I really needed to know. The other members that left in the two vans would not be returning until at least dark. All I can do is wait. I sat there a few hours thinking of a plan to find out if she was in there. Or was I watching an empty house. I almost walked up to the front door and knocked. Boy was I bored. I had to go off of my experience dealing with this cult and think of what I was not thinking about. Yes, I said that. I had to rely on what I did know. This cult would never leave their members alone for any reason. Either she was in the house with someone or she had been taken somewhere at night.

I decided to take a chance and do something I had not done since I was a kid. With the curtains in their house shut I could not see in, and that meant they could not see out. I went up and rang the doorbell and ran like hell. It took a few minutes before I saw the curtain open up far enough to see Gerri's face. Shortly after that the door opened and a male stuck his head out. Well that answered that question. I knew these two were not going anywhere today without a vehicle. There is not any reason to hang around and take the chance the police would show up. I am in a neighborhood watch area, and I did not want to be questioned. I went back to my room and got caught up with a much-needed rest. My alarm went off and I was not ready to get up yet, but I had to. I drove back to the house and it was starting to get dark. I parked in my favorite spot. Within an hour both vans pulled into the driveway. Gerri came out of the house probably out of sheer boredom. She did not come off the porch, and a minute or two later a sports car pulled up out front of the house. One person got out of the car and walked past all the kids standing in the driveway. He went straight up to Gerri and started talking to her. None of the other cult members approached them. It was like they knew to stay away for some reason. The cult kids that had just gotten out of the vans did not enter the house through the front door that was closer to them; they walked around to the side door and went inside. Whatever this guy was saying to Gerri was private. They talked for some time considering it was cold as heck outside. The guy that was talking to Gerri was no doubt a team leader. A couple minutes later he walked off the porch and got into his car and drove off. That was weird. I wish I could have heard that conversation. What was going on and why was Gerri not with the rest of the cult kids out soliciting? It just did not make any sense. I have been on a lot of Moonie cases and this was not right. What was going to happen next, who knows? What I was sure of was I needed to get back to my room and grab my things and check out. Something was about to happen, and I needed to be here to find out what. I got back as quick as I could, and I was not leaving until I unfolded this next event. Things stayed quiet all night and it was morning.

I had been up all night. I did not want to miss anything. The same thing happened again. After the two vans were warmed up, all the cult kids got into their vans and drove off, without Gerri. Well I do believe I am going to be awake all day. By this time, I was totally confused. I did not stay that way for long. A few minutes later the same sports car that was here the night before pulled up and he made no attempt to blow his horn. Within seconds Gerri walked out of the house got into his car and they drove off. I followed. We drove for what seemed forever. It took all day, but we were back in New York City. They pulled into an awfully expensive hotel, and a valet parked their car. Both of them had travel bags. I got lucky and found a parking spot, and it was only one million dollars a day. I took it any way. I was back in New York City and I guess that was the going rate. Things started to become a little clearer now, and I was ready for anything. I took a room in the same hotel and I am not even going to say how much that cost. I did not care. I was beyond tired; I had been running on my third wind for some time now. I wanted to stay close to these two. After checking into my room, I sat there and put everything together that I knew the best I could. This is what I came up with. Something happened during Gerri's camping excursion, and her leader was brought in to make it right. Either she was having doubts about the group or the cult found out about her parents' money. Either way at that moment I did not think I would ever see Gerri again. It was just a feeling. I was hoping I was wrong. The cult was going to pamper her. This hotel proved that. Well I was happy to eat something that did not come out of a bag or a tin can. I sat for the longest time thinking about what my next move was going to be. I knew following someone in this city was going to be almost impossible without being noticed. I just did not feel right about what was going on. In the back of my mind I knew what the cult had in store for her, and it was going to take place back in San Francisco at the farm. What was I going to do to stop this from happening? What I did find out I will tell you later in the story. My plan was to continue to do what I was good at, and that was to keep following them until I had the chance to remove her from the cult. But was this enough, and would I have enough time. Stay tuned. This plan was going to be a lot harder to do than usual.

If they decide to stay in the city, I will bring in the rest of my team in case there is a chance to grab her. If they would leave the city, it would be a little easier. It would take them a few days to travel from New York to San Francisco and that would give us the time I needed to make this work. I know what you are thinking and yes, I have thought about if they were to fly there. I could have a team at the airport before their plane would touch down. Either way I had to know what they were going to do before they did it. That part I had to work on. I believed the next day would tell. I got up early and I was waiting in my car for them to come out. I had a good view of the front of the hotel, and if the valet would bring their car around, they would have to drive right past me. I was all set. I thought if I could have only brought in my team last night, we could make this work today. But there was not enough time. It was getting late and I had not seen them yet. I was starting to think I was right about never seeing Gerri again. I could not let myself think this way, I needed to stay positive.

It was now past check out time and I was really starting to get concerned. The thought crossed my mind that I had gotten outsmarted. After I calmed myself down, I thought about the possibility of them staying over for another night or maybe they were just running late. His car was still sitting in the same spot that it was parked in last night.

I always felt that I was fairly good at my job and I really care about these kids. I do believe it helps me in my decision making. The problem was I knew something was not right. It had not been right for some time. I made the decision to go into the hotel and have a look around. I could not take the chance that I could miss them inside, so I ripped up one of my perfectly good t shirts, and I shoved them up the exhaust pipes of his sports car. I knew this would not stop them, but it was sure going to slow them down. After that I looked around in the restaurant but no Gerri or her bodyguard. Yes, I said bodyguard. I was not dealing with her cult leader anymore. He had been replaced by a bodyguard. This is what I found out earlier. I found out her cult leader had been waiting at the hotel all this time for her to arrive. The man that drove her to the city was her bodyguard. I was not going to find her anywhere in New York City. She had been flown out last night. I needed to be one hundred per cent sure. I was not worried about being seen at this point, because in the back of my mind I knew there was not anyone here that I needed to hide from anymore.

I took the elevator up to the floor they were staying on, and when I got to their room the maid was in there cleaning it. I asked her if this party had checked out, and she said she was not sure, but there were no bags left behind. This is what I had expected. There was one more thing I needed to do to satisfied myself. I went down to the front desk, and I told the woman behind the counter that I was supposed to meet my party from three twelve here to take a flight out this morning, and I was running late. Did I miss them? She checked and she told me they had taken the hotel shuttle last night to the airport. I knew it. I had to tell myself that even if I would have seen them leave last night, I would not have been able to stop them. I did not need to know where they were going. I already knew. I was totally heartbroken. I had let Gerri and her family down, and that is a hard thing to come to grips with. When I look back on things, I am not sure there would have been a good safe time to grab her even if I would have had my team with me. At least that is what I had to tell myself. Who knows? I called the Parkers and told them what had happened. I told them they would be receiving a call in the near future from Gerri. She would be calling to try to drain as much money she could from her parents. The cult would make sure of that. I explained to them I did the best I could to remove her from the cult, but my best was not good enough. The cult had gotten wind of her parent's money, and they were sending Gerri back to their farm, until she was stripped of all her beliefs in normal society. This is what is called Brain Washing. I went on to tell the Parkers she would be making that phone call home, but it was going to take a while. I instructed them on what to do and say when that happened. I assured them we would be ready when that time comes. We were going to have another shot at removing Gerri from the cult, and that made me feel a little better. Not much. I was feeling bad for what I knew Gerri was going to go through over the next few weeks and that made me sad. I cannot give you the end result of what became of Gerri. We never did receive a call back from Gerri's parents. The word on the street was she was removed from the cult by the other team on the west coast. No matter how hard we try we just cannot win them all. But that does not mean we would not keep on trying. I got outsmarted by the cult this time, but it would never happen again.

CHAPTER SEVEN

CHILDREN OF GOD: CHRISTINE

This story is about an incredibly beautiful woman I am going to call Christine. Christine had gotten caught up in a religious cult by the name of Children of God. It was founded by a man by the name of David Berg. At one time the government had rated this group of one of the most dangerous cult groups around. Berg had plans for Christine. She was being used to recruit new members. She had succumbed to mind control and had been with the group for some time now. What my readers need to know is, the primary belief of this group is sex with children is not only ok but is their given right. If we were going to be successful in removing Christine from this cult it will be a big blow to their organization. Christine was valuable to Berg.

Along with sex with children there was sex everywhere. Prostitution was one of the ways the cult would bring in money for the group. We had already done the surveillance and had Christine in our car and were heading for our safe house. Now our deprogrammer could start to untwist the damage that had been done to Christine. We arrived at our safe house without any trouble. The deprogrammer that we were using to help Christine was on loan to us from another group that did the same kind of work we did. I had heard his methods were a little different, but how different, I did not know. He was supposed to be good but was he good enough? We have always had our own standers and our rules we followed.

When the deprogrammer arrived at our location he was brought into Christine's room. This deprogrammer I am going to give him the name of Gutless. You will find out later why I chose that name for him. After meeting with Christine, he pulled me aside and told me he was going to work with Christine by himself. I told him that was against our rules and he said he did not care. I told him I would go alone with his request if the door to Christine room was always left open. Part of my job is to keep up with the progress of Christine's deprogramming. It is left up to me to transport Christine to our rehab center when she was deprogrammed successfully. I would not transport anyone unless I was sure they had been successfully deprogramed. I went on to tell Gutless if Christine would decide to get violent with him, we would not be able to help in time. He said he did not care. He was dead set of being the only one in Christine room. At least one of our security guys would be sitting in the doorway of Christine's room at all times. We were in the second week of the deprograming and Christine had been behaving herself. By the third week she was starting to show doubts about the cult she belonged to. He was getting through to her. Two days later she denounced the cult. It seemed like he had done his job. He decided to spend a couple more days with Christine and I was glad to hear that. The next day he asked me to make travel arrangements and I told him I would. I had always trusted my gut when it came to be doing my job. For what I had heard and seen it looked like she had been deprogrammed successfully.

The next day we drove to the airport and had already gone through security. Everything was going well, and Christine was talking with her mother. They were making plans and things were looking normal. We walked over to an area next door to the bar/ restaurant and Gutless got up and went to the bathroom. Christine ask one of my security if she could have something to eat and he said yes. I asked the mother if she would sit still until Gutless came back from the bathroom and then they were to meet us next door. She said she would. I only needed one other security guy with me to transport Christine to rehab, so I sent the other security home earlier.

We had just sat down when Gutless and Christine's mother came in and joined us. For some reason I would find out later why, he started yelling at the top of his voice. He was directing his anger towards me. The problem was I was not the one that was going to be affected by his tone. The words that came out of his mouth explained his anger. He said how dare you bring my girlfriend in here. Then he shut up. He realized what he said, and he did not mean to say it, at least not out loud. That is what I had been missing. Since I was not allowed to sit in on Christine's deprogramming, I would have seen it happing. He was in love with Christine all in three weeks. Christine was an exceptionally beautiful young lady and I can see how someone could get caught up in her beauty, but it was very unprofessional of him. I kick myself every time I think about that day. I still should have seen it happening. But I did not. What happened next, I had seen before, and when I saw it before I said I never wanted to see it again. Yes, it was that bad. Christine's eyes glazed over, and her skin turned pale, and before I could stand up, she took off running through the airport. I was right behind her with my other security guy on my heels. Even Christine's mother was following behind us. Christine ran for a while before she ended up at the feet of an excessively big policeman. By the time I caught up with her she was telling the officer she had been kidnaped. Needless to say, I did not really know what to do next. This has never happened before. To make things worst we were in the Atlanta airport. Over the last year someone had been kidnaping little black children and so far, they have been unable to catch them. Things were not looking good. All I could think about was being charged with kidnapping. Maybe we might. By this time two other officers joined us. Were handcuffs coming next? I handed my badge to the officer and started to explain what was going on. The next thing I knew we were being loaded into a van and on our way to the police station. All of us were put into the same van, and I knew I had to do something.

I did not waste any time in attempting to untwist what this deprogrammer had gotten us into. Are you asking where is Gutless during this time? He disappeared somewhere. I found out later he got on another flight. He took off and left us holding the bag. I kept on talking to Christine. I was not a trained deprogrammer, but I had been working with them for years. I had to give it a shot. There was no one else. I told her do not throw away all she had learned over the last few days. She sat and stared at her mother. I was happy to see she had not started chanting yet. This was a good thing. I was hoping her mother would be a factor in what she would do next. I continued to talk with her all the way to the police station and after we arrived. We were taken into a small room and told to sit down. I kept on talking with her. Sitting across the table from us was a police officer. What he did surprised me. He just sat there and did not say a word. He was letting me talk to Christine with no interruptions. He knew what was going on and I could tell he was trying to be on our side. He did not like religious cults, and he was tired of running them out of the airport. She started to respond to what I was saying and at one point I got a smile out of her. She started to talk with me instead of just sitting there. I felt given the time I could get her to come back with us. Part of Christine wanted to go home with her mother and there is that other part that did not. I needed to get rid of the other part. Things seemed to be going as good as it could and the whole time the officer sat there and sad nothing. She asked the officer if she could use the bathroom and he said yes. They started to walk towards the door, and I stood up and asked if I could go along and he said no. I knew right then I would lose what I had accomplished with her. They were gone for some time. It was taking to long for her to return and I knew what she had done. I got that answer a few minutes later. When they returned her eyes were dilated and her skin was pail. This was not a good sign. She sat down in between her mother and myself and I started my conversation with her again. Unfortunately, I was not getting through to her. She had the chance to chant and it returned her state of mind back to an awfully bad place. We had not been charged with any crime up to this point. But was all that going to change? I was out of time and I knew it. What Christine did when she went to the bathroom was to make a call to her cult leader. I knew what that meant. I turned to the officer and asked him to keep everyone from her cult away from her. I told him she was not in her right mind, and if he had any doubts to ask her mother that was sitting there. She stood up and pleaded with him to release her into her custody. It was a shot in the dark, but there was not anything else to do. The officer said he could not do that. Her cult leader walked into the room and said a couple words to her, and it was over. I had lost her. All my thoughts were concentrated on her mother. She was probably never going to see her daughter again. This cult group will make sure of that. I knew what her mother was going to go through over the next few weeks. There was not anything I could do to make things better. Christine said to the officer she would not bring any charges against us if she was free to go. I continued to try to get across to the officer to not let this happen. I knew trying to get through to Christine was not going to happen. My last shot was hoping to convince the officer this was a family issue and nothing else. He was not buying it. He told me he had the right to hold us on charges of kidnapping. I decided to stop trying. He was giving us a chance to walk away from this, but it was a tradeoff. Lose Christine and we would go free. When Christine and her cult leader walked out the door my heart broke. It still hurts when I think about this story, but it was a story that needed to be told. It only goes to show how powerful and dangerous mind control is.

Christine was not in her right mind, that was obvious. The officers saw it, but he could not do any more to help. I feel I should have seen this happening from the beginning, but I did not. I keep telling myself I am only human, but I knew that was only an excuse. Her mother was devastated. She brought Christine into this world and now she has chosen to walk away from her. I told her mother it was not Christine that was making that decision, it was the mind control. I could not let her mother go home and be by herself, so I took her back to my home where she was welcomed by my family. She stayed with us for two weeks until she could find some understanding on what just happened. As far as I know Christine never did go back home and for that my heart goes out to her mother. No parent should ever have to go through what she did. This is one of those stories that remind us that we are not perfect. We cannot see and hear everything.

To Christine's mother if you read this, I will always have an empty space in my heart. Hopefully, Christine held on to that small part of her that wanted to return with her mother. I pray she found a way to do so. I still carry the sadness of losing her and I probably will for some time to come. As a parent myself there is not anything in this world more precious than our children. As for Gutless you know who you are, what comes around goes around. Remember that. Now you can see why I chose that name for him. He was very unprofessional, and I hope he does not forget about Christine and her mother. No one knows if he would have stayed with us, could he have a made a difference in the life of Christine and her family. The problem was he did not give her the chance and we will never know.

CHAPTER EIGHT

MOONIE CULT: WHISKERS

This story takes me out of the United States and into Canada. My office got a call from Becky who is a member of a parent group. We were being asked if we would go out of the country, into Canada and help a family whose son had gotten caught up in the Moonies. His name is Whiskers. We were being asked to leave right away. Whiskers was coming home to collect the inheritance his grandfather had left him. Whiskers was due home in five days. Sara, my office guru, informed me she did not have anyone that could leave right away. I placed a call to Whiskers mother to get the information she had. She said her son joined the cult and he has not been seen since. She had me hooked when she said inheritance. I knew what that meant.

We needed to do something to stop that from happening. Once he got his hands on his money, he would turn it all over to the cult. All two million dollars. I had been down this road to many times before. With any luck we could put an end to this before it begins. I told Sara I was going to Canada and see if I could help. I placed a call to Whiskers mother and told her to expect me later that day.

The wheels in my head were turning and I had an idea to remove him from the cult. This would be the first time anyone would attempt to do a deprogramming in Canada. I do not believe it had been tried before. Sara booked me a flight out and after arriving I met with all fifteen of Whiskers family. Everyone was there, cousins, sisters, aunts, and uncles, and even the neighbor. This was the largest group of family members that has ever shown up for a deprogramming, I had ever seen. They all wanted to help in any way they could. I sat and listened to each and every one of them talk. I did not have the heart at that time to tell them that I might be the only one to show up to help them. There was not time to wait for Sara to get me some help. My plan was to use Whiskers family members as my security team. It sounded crazy to me too and it may turn out to be. We were all crammed into the Living room and talking about what needed to be done. I needed at least ten people that knew what they were doing to have the chance to pull this off. If Sara does come through for me then everything should go smooth. I could tell Whiskers family members were close.

I got with Bill, Whiskers father and told him what I was going to need from him. He said whatever was needed he would try. I asked him to have ten of his trusted family members here in the morning. Bill invited me to stay the night and I accepted.

I did not get much sleep last night. I was doing way too much thinking. I had little time to put this together and I was not too sure I wanted to do this without my regular crew. The opportunity we had in front of us, we could not ignore. It is not every day a cult kid comes home for any reason. I cannot pass it up. I must make this work, especially with this much money at stake. Besides, I do not want to see Whiskers spend any more time with this cult. The next morning came early. I never told Bill what time to have everyone here in the morning. At five am they were walking through the door with coffee and donuts. They were very eager. I sat down with them and explained I was still hoping that Sara would come through for me, but if she did not, I was going to move forward with his family members. I needed two family members to detain Whiskers cult leader. He would not be coming home alone. I was hoping he did not bring any more of his cult leaders with him. I needed to plan for more. I put Bill in charge of who was best to handle what task. I went on to explain what to expect from his cult leader. I told them at no time where they permitted to use violence. Only restrain. They said ok. I told them if we did this right, we could control the violence that may occur.

I told everyone when Whiskers and his leader walked through the door everyone needed to be out of sight except for myself, the father, and the mother. I was going to need four family members in the bedroom and two more in the attached garage. I would be sitting on the edge of the couch in case they would get spooked and try to leave. Once they stepped into the house the mother was to greet her son just like she always did. She was to introduce me as the reader of the will. Then I would walk slowly towards the kitchen. I would say to Whiskers I had everything set up in the kitchen for the reading of the will. Then I would ask him if we could get started so I could make my daughters basketball game in an hour. I was counting on Whiskers to follow behind me. I was thinking his cult leader was not going to let him go into the kitchen alone. I was going to tell his leader no one except family was allowed in the same room when the will was read. I would tell him to sit down and relax, this is not going to take exceptionally long. He needed to be sitting for this to work smoothly. Once he was sitting the mother would ask if anyone wanted something to drink. That was the cue for the two family members to walk up next to his leader and make sure he did not get up. Hopefully, he was going to be the only person the cult would send home with him. I allowed for more just in case. I had two more family members in the other bedroom. While all this was happening Whiskers and I would be alone in the kitchen. When I stomped my foot that was the cue for the other two family members to walk through the garage door and stand on either side of Whiskers. I informed all the family members to not get into a conversation with Whiskers. I did not want to deal with anything other than getting him out of this house and into the safe house the father had set up for us. The mother was instructed to go into the garage and get into the front seat of our rental car and wait for us. I would tell Whiskers we had some people here that wanted to talk with him, and he needed to stay calm. I would go on and tell him we were going for a ride. The father was instructed to tell his cult leader he would be free to go after we had gone, if he behaved himself.

Whiskers would be escorted into the garage and put into the back seat of my rental car. That would give us one person on either side of Whiskers, the mother in the front seat and I would be driving. Hopefully, our deprogrammers would be at the safe house waiting for us. The father was instructed to stay behind for one hour before he let his cult leader go. Then he was instructed to meet up with us. This was the plan and it seemed that everyone was ready. I went on to say again that I was hoping that the rest of my team would show up in time. They understood. We would be ready if they did not. This will be the first time I have ever attempted to do this without my regular crew. I was extremely nervous. I did receive some good news from Sara. Two deprogrammers were in route to my location. They should arrive the next day. This was big. One of the deprogrammers that was coming was also a backup security guy. Things were starting to come together. In two days, Whiskers would be coming home. Up to this point I was feeling ok with using his family members as my crew, but there was no way of knowing if anyone of them would freeze up in the middle of this operation. I am fairly good at my job, and everyone had their roles to play, but things could easily get out of control if just one person hesitates to do his part. The one thing I had going for me was we were going to do this at the parents' home, and that gives me a sense of relief. If something should go wrong at least we should be able to contain it inside their home. I explained to everyone it is important to me that no one gets hurt. The deprogramming staff is top notch, and it is the job of the security to keep everyone safe.

That evening I got a call from Sara. There was an issue with getting the security staff here in time. They were flying in from two different states, and two of them would not be here until the morning when Whiskers was due to come home. It was going to be close. I shifted my back up guys around to accommodate my crew arriving. Things were looking up from when it first started. As time got closer to the day, I could tell that some of his family members were having doubts about what they were being asked to do. I was not too concerned until Bill told me we would be losing three of his family members. There was not any time to replace them now. Things were not looking so good. Even though I had people on their way, I could not count on them until they were standing in front of me. Not only did I have to count on their planes coming in on time, but they had to get through customs. I was not so concerned that no one had ever tried a deprogramming in Canada, it was getting through customs afterwards that was a concern. Well there is a first time for everything.

The two deprogrammers arrived in time, and I took one of them to our safe house and dropped him off. I got the other one up to speed on what we were trying to do. He said he had not heard of anyone attempting to do a deprogramming in Canada and then crossing the border into the USA. He went on to say that doing this without our regular guys was crazy. But he said he was in. I was pleased to hear that. I was going to need everyone to get on board if we were to do this successfully. One of the other security guys had made it through customs and he was on his way. All we need now was two more security guys and we would have the team back together. It was Friday a.m. and I just received a call from the other security guys. They should be arriving within the hour. It was seven o'clock in the morning and I knew Whiskers would be on his way at any time now. It was unclear how far away the Moonie house was that Whiskers was staying in. We had no clue on how long of a drive he would have ahead of him. I knew it was cutting it close. We all stood around and watched the clock. Boy was that nerve racking. You could cut the tension in the air with a knife. I told my other two guys to honk the horn when they arrived. One of us would be looking out for them. I did not need them walking through the front door if Whiskers was ahead of them. It would cause too much commotion. They were instructed to enter through the garage. We were as ready as we could be. Now who was going to walk through the door first? Whickers or the rest of my staff. We waited.

Shortly after eight we heard a car horn. It was coming from down the street. My guys were here. I was hoping that Whiskers had not arrived at the same time and they would be walking up the street at the same time. That is what was going through my head. Things were running to close for comfort. Whiskers should be arriving with a shaved head and a ponytail. None of my security staff had the chance to see a picture of Whiskers. There had not been enough time. When my two teammates walked through the door, I got the biggest smile on my face. They took their positions without anyone saying a word to them. They were that good. All of us had been through this so many times it came natural to us. I gathered the rest of Whiskers family members together and I thanked them for stepping up to help. We did not need them now. I asked them to stay in the bedroom until we had Whiskers out of the house. I explained it was too much of a risk if one of them would get in the way of us making this work. They said they understood. A few more minutes a car pulled up out front, it was him and he was not alone. His cult leader came with him. We were all set. They entered through the front door and shut the door behind them. I just needed them to walk five more feet and everything would be in place. They did. The mother did a great job, and everything was going as planned. I went through my speech and I started walking towards the kitchen and Whiskers did not follow me, he was in front of me. Things were going well. His leader must have been through a few of these readings before because he walked over and sat down. The mother was right on time. She asked if anyone wanted something to drink, and out popped my two security guys. By now they were standing over his leader. He started to get up and they told him to sit down. That is just what he did. We had no problem with either one of them. I escorted Whiskers to the garage and put him into the back seat. His mother was already in the front seat. He continued to stay quiet even when we took him into the safe house. And, as promised, the father let his cult leader go and he joined us at the safe house. Whiskers did what all cults do when they are removed from their cult, and that was to chant. It was not until five days later that he spoke a word to anyone. He was eating well. He had been taught to resist. He must have not got that memo because he was eating everything he was given. Some of his family members were staying in the house but they were not allowed to see him until it was time. The deprogrammers kept on doing their magic, quoting from the Bible and it was not long before he started coming around.

He would come to see that the things the cult had told him were not true. He was a bright boy and it was not long before he was asking a lot of questions. A few days later the deprogrammers had broken through the mind control and he was on his way back to his own self. I got together with all fifteen family members and brought them in for a visit with Whiskers. You should have seen all of them together hugging and kissing, crying, and laughing. It was wonderful to see. Like usual I made travel arrangements to go to rehab. I asked Whiskers if he was ready to go to the USA for a vacation and he said sure. The night before we were to leave for the US the deprogrammer asked Whiskers if he was ready to get his ponytail cut off and he said he was ready. This is the last test they would use to check how well he was doing. Remember in an earlier story the Moonies believe that the only way to get to heaven was for Moon to lift them up by their ponytails. This was a big step. The deprogrammer asked me to hand him the scissors, so I did. The deprogrammers took the scissors and reached around and grabbed his tail. All the security staff was watching. What he did next shocked all of us. He handed the scissors to Whiskers. He took them and then he looked me square in the eyes and then he smiled. I thought I was going to be cut again. I had been cut before and I really did not want to go through that again. I was closer to him than anyone else, so I figured it was going to be me. After he smiled, he reached back and cut his pony tail off. Then he handed the scissors to me and smiled again. You could hear a pin drop when the deprogrammer handed him the scissors. There was no doubt the deprogrammers had done their job. He was successfully deprogramed. After that was over, I got with the deprogramming team and told them if they were ever thinking about doing that again to at least warn me. They just laughed and said sure. We were all set to leave for the good old USA the next day. Whiskers spent the whole night talking to his family members making plans for after rehab. The last and final test was going through customs. The next day came early. I sent home the security staff that would not be needed to transport him and his family to rehab. It was time to leave for our trip. We decided to drive to the US and then pick up a flight from there. As we pulled up to the entrance to the border patrol, they ordered us to park and grab our bags and to enter their building.

Well here we go on that trip I was not looking forward to. We did what we were told to do. There was Whiskers, his parents, two deprogrammers and three security guys. We walked into the building and we were told to put our bags on the table and take a seat. The officer in charge had our ids and he was studying them closely. What he said next was hard to answer. He asked how did so many people from so many different places get together in Canada. And how do we know each other. No one said a word. I started to speak up, not knowing what I was going to say, when one of the other officers that was going through our bags interrupted me. He had in his hand a piece of paper that should have been left at home or thrown away. He asked who owns this briefcase. One of the deprogrammers said it was his. The man in charge motioned to this officer to handcuff the deprogrammer and to take him into a different room. The piece of paper he was holding up was a subpoena for the deprogrammer to show up in court for kidnapping. I could not believe what was happening. I wanted to curl up in the corner and disappear. I figured something was going to happen but not this. We all just stood there in silence. I knew what was going on in everyone's head, we had talked about this many times before and we all knew this could happen. I was thinking we would be locked up and never see the light of day. Not only were we going to be charged with kidnapping, but we would be turned over to US customs and we would be charged in that country also.

I needed to do something. I decided the truth was going to be our best shot. I spoke up and explained that we were hired by Whiskers parents to come to Canada and have a talk with their son. He stood up and said you mean deprogram their son. I answered back yes, some people would call it that. He turned to Whiskers mother and asked if this was true and she said yes. A few minutes later he told Whiskers and his parents to go into this other room and wait for him. Then the same officer whispered something into the other officer's ear. He walked over and locked the door. The officer in charged walked into the room with the family and shut the door. At that point in time I was not worried about myself, I was concerned for Whiskers. I was hoping he was strong enough to not want to go back to the cult. Only time would tell.

It seemed like they were in that room forever. When the door finally opened the first person that walked through the door was Whiskers. He was smiling. Ok now was this a good smile or a bad one. It was not until he gave us the thumbs up, we knew what he meant. Everyone was looking at each other and wondering what was going to happen next. I had been keeping an eye on the clock. We had a flight to catch and it was an hour drive and we had forty-five minutes to do it in. That is if we were going to be let off the hook. None of us knew. All we knew was Whiskers was happy, and he was still sitting across the room from us. The man in charge walked out and whispered something in the other officer's ear again, and then he left the room. Then he turned to us and said I should throw all of you in jail for what we were trying to get away with. Then he went silent. Just as he started to talk the door opened and out walked our deprogrammer without handcuffs on. The officer said we were free to go but to never come across the border on his shift again. I asked him if we could leave right away because we had a flight to catch and truly little time to do so. He said to get the heck out of there before he changed his mind.

When we walked out the door, we all turned to Whiskers and thanked him. If it was not for him, we were on our way to jail. He just smiled. I was starting to like his smile. We all were.

It was not over yet. We had a long way to go and little time to do it in. One of the other security guys was driving and he knew our situation. It was imperative that we made our flight and he knew it. Shortly after hopping in our car we were traveling over one hundred miles per hour. What we did not know was a couple hundred yards down the road the Canadians had set up radar. We all saw the officer sitting in his car as we blew by him going over the speed limit by a lot. He did not pursue us. I honestly believe that the officer at the border patrol radioed ahead we would be flying by and not to stop us. There was just no other explanation. We did make our flight thanks to our driver. And we were all glad to have our feet on the ground in the good old USA. We did get Whiskers and both of his parents to our rehab and all three of them are doing well. After rehab they returned to Canada and Whiskers did not returned to the cult.

We all got together to do something that had never been done before, and we pulled it off, thanks to our teammates, Whiskers parents and the border patrol that overlooked something that was really important to us. And thanks to Whiskers for being strong enough to know the difference between right and wrong.

CHAPTER NINE

MOONIE CULT: TEDDY

I had been in Colorado for about a week on vacation, and just walked in from rafting the Colorado River. The first thing I did was check my answering machine and there was a message from my boss. I will call him C. He requested I get to San Francisco as soon as possible. I caught a flight out the next day. Upon my arrival I was briefed by C. He told me we were in pursuit of a young male twenty years old from Arizona. I was informed I was being called in to replace one of our security guys that had not had any luck in locating this young man, I will call Teddy.

He had spent ten days searching for Teddy and he was not any closer to locating him. Time was running out. It is not uncommon to spend a few weeks searching for someone that has gotten caught up in a Religious Cult. To my understanding, Teddy was just another one of your typical Moonie victims. He was going to turn twenty-one years old in a couple of weeks and he had plans to turn over his inheritance of over two million dollars to the cult. Needless to say, he was not going to be easy to find. The cult would make sure of that.

The first thing I had to do after meeting with C was to meet with Teddy's parents. I drove over to their motel and talked with them for a short time. The father met me at the door, and the first thing out of his mouth was," what are you going to do that the other security guy could not do?" I stood there for a few seconds and said," find your son". Teddy's father walked over and sat down and said nothing. Teddy's mother walked up to me and gave me a hug and she said," I know you will". I listened to what they had to say. I told them I needed to get out onto the streets and find their son. As I left their room, I questioned why I put so much pressure on myself by telling them I would find their son. There are no guarantees in this business, but I felt it needed to be said. All I needed to do now was to follow through with my promise.

It was not going to be easy to find Teddy with that much money on the line. The cult would be keeping him well guarded. There was not any reason to look on the streets for Teddy. He would not be soliciting. I passionately believed he would not be working at all. The cult is going to pamper him until all his money is transferred to their bank account. Then he will be put on the streets to solicit just like everyone else that is under Moons mind control. I went over the list of places C had given me that had already been checked for Teddy. There was not any time for me to revisit his footsteps. I needed another approach. I decided to start my search at a health food store owned by the Moonies. This store is located down the street from their house, where all the new recruits go for dinner. It was not on the list of places that had been checked. It was a good place to start.

This store is uncharted territory for our group. It is new. I took a stroll down the street to have a look around. Once I arrived, I found there was no place to set up any kind of surveillance without being discovered. The rear entrance to the store was fenced in and was only opened for deliveries. This was not going to be easy. I could not take the chance of blowing my cover this early in my search. Going into the store was out of the question. I had no way of knowing if he was in there or not. It was a good place for them to hide him without him realizing they were doing so. I decided to check out a couple of other places that were not on the list. Two days had gone by and I was not getting any closer to finding Teddy. Sometimes we try too hard to do something we want so bad; we miss what is right in front of us. It did not take me exceptionally long to figure out what needed to be done. It was a long shot. Done wrong it would be dangerous. I was going to need some back up in case something went wrong. I called C for some assistance and told him what I wanted to do. He agreed. It was my plan to infiltrate into the Moonies and hope Teddy would show up for dinner. It was a long shot. But it is the only one I had.

There are a lot of potential prospects hanging around downtown, and at Fisherman's Wharf. It was Friday afternoon and I strolled down to Fisherman's Wharf to get my invitation to dinner. As I stood under their billboard looking at the pictures of their farm, I got my invitation to dinner. It was late enough in the day for the bus to arrive to take us all to dinner. All forty of us. Yes, I said forty. I told you this was a prime spot for the cult to recruit.

We all loaded the bus and took the short ride to dinner.

Once we arrived, we were escorted into the house and told, not asked, to remove our shoes. We walked up the steps and were told to wait there for dinner instructions. No one knew that when we removed our shoes downstairs a cult member moved them into a different room. This was done to stop anyone who would decide to try to leave early. It is just another plan in the scheme of things the cult uses to have full control over everyone. As soon as we were led into the dining room, I was approached by an incredibly beautiful young lady who was one of Moons recruiters. She grabbed my arm and led me down a hallway to an area that had four closed doors. She was talking the whole time as we walked. Her conversation was all about the farm. She led me into one of the rooms that contained a piano. She sat down and started to play, making sure I stayed close. I sat there and listened while she played. She continued to talk about the farm while she was playing. What she did not know was I could not be any more disinterested in what she said. I was anxious to look around for Teddy. I stood up in the attempt to look around and she grabbed my arm and sat me back down. I did not want to look too disinterested in her, so I played along. About that time, we were called to dinner. She walked me out of the room never letting go of my arm. During dinner she stayed right beside me. After dinner, everyone was gathered in a circle, and they started to sing. Again, she held on tight. Up to this point I had not seen anyone else other than the cult staff and the group that had joined us for dinner. Time was running out. I was incredibly lucky to have talked to C before I entered the house for dinner. The information he had given me became valuable.

After the singing was over, they started the short film about the farm. I knew I needed to get out of there before the film ended. It was going to be a lot harder for me to leave after the film was over without making a scene. Their security staff was already here. They were probably behind those closed doors. The film had been running for a few minutes and I was running out of time. One of the doors opened down the hallway and out walked a large gentleman. The big guy walked past all of us and stopped at the top of the stairs. It was time for me to leave. I was not getting on that bus. I still needed to keep somewhat of a low profile because I had not found Teddy and my time had run out. There was still a chance to locate him, but I needed to get out of there safely. That was not going to be easy with that big guy at the top of the stairs. Do not forget my friend on the end of my arm. Yep, she was not letting go. I decided it was time. I started walking towards the steps with her in tow. When I reached the top of the steps, I excused myself around the big fellow, with her still holding on for dear life. Both of us walked around the big guy and he turned the other way and just stood there. The only reason he let me go around him was because the girl on my arm was a cult recruiter.

As soon as I got around him, I broke loose from her grasp and headed down the stairs. I did not look back to see if I was being followed, still wanting enough time to look around downstairs. I was going to wait until I got to the bottom of the steps to make that decision. I had gotten fairly good at knowing if someone was behind me or not, and so far, no one was. I still had to deal with the fact there could be more security downstairs through one of the doors that entered the house. I was not ready to deal with that quite yet. When I got halfway down the steps and looked up, there, at the bottom of the stairs was Teddy, and two of his bodyguards. I could not believe what I was seeing, or was it really him? I had a picture of him I got from C when I showed up a few days ago. Having a chance to look at it a few times, I was doubting what I was seeing. I wanted it to be him. Did I want it so bad that my mind was thinking it was him? I needed to be sure. They started walking up the steps as I was walking down. I reached into my pocket and pulled out my two-way radio. I put it up to my ear as I walked by him. I said to no one on the other end of my radio," yes Teddy, I will call you when I get home". When I said that, Teddy looked up as to acknowledge he had heard his name. Ok, now was I going to be able to get past his security team that was a couple steps behind him? Only time would tell. It seemed like those few seconds were hours. We just kept on walking. When I reached the bottom of the steps, I walked out the door. I needed to get out of there for a couple of reasons. One reason was because I was so happy to have found Teddy, I could not get the smile off my face, and two I needed to report that I did locate him. I got lucky. Having that young girl on the end of my arm at the time she was with me was big. For any of Moons security guys to not do their job was my good luck. He would not have let me past him without confronting me if she were not on my arm. That was his job. As I have said before, all of Moons puppets do what they are told. I got lucky.

Well, there I was with no shoes on and standing in the middle of the street. Boy, did I look stupid. I had no intentions of going back into the house to retrieve my shoes. I had located Teddy and for that I was thrilled. My work was not done by a long shot. I needed to know if he was going to get on the bus with the rest of the dinner guests or not. I ripped off my socks and ran up the street. It felt surprisingly good to put some distance between me and their security team. I went into a corner store and bought two newspapers. I quickly headed back towards the Moonie house. I needed to see everyone who got on the bus. The problem was the bus had tinted windows, and the only way to see into the bus was to be on the side of the bus where the door was. Unfortunately, the door was on the other side. I went around the other side of the bus and sat down on the sidewalk close enough to see who was going to get on the bus. With the newspapers draped over me and having no shoes on, I fit right in with all the other weirdos that were on the streets for the night. The film had stopped playing and any minute they would be loading the bus for the farm. I just sat there and waited. After everyone that was getting on the bus had done so the bus drove off. Teddy was not with them. I was almost in the clear for the night. I got up and went back up the street to keep an eye on the house.

I had to be sure Teddy was not going to be moved to another location. It took some time for the lights in the house to go out. It was already past dark, and I was mentally and physically tired. I believed they were all in for the night, so I was able to return to my room and rest. The first thing I did was call C to let him know I had found Teddy and how. He was pleased. I asked him to call Teddy's parents and tell them. I was just too tired to sit and talk with anyone tonight. I knew they would be relieved. Well up to now I had done my job. I had found Teddy and I had done it in a short amount of time. My work had just begun, but it was all I could do for the night. I rested soundly and would be back at the Moonie house before daylight. It was Saturday morning and the shops that were up and down the street from the Moonie house were not going to be open until nine. I was able to park my rental car up the street from their house. I sat in my car until the lights in the house came on. It was shortly before nine. Shoppers started to arrive, and I was going to need them if I was going to blend in.

I was happy having my car so close to me so I could follow if Teddy were taken from the house. I decided to go back to the little store where I picked up the newspapers the night before and get a cup of coffee. After getting my coffee I walked outside to the corner where I could get a good look at the house. Now that I had located Teddy what I needed to do was to follow him around to get his routine down. Then I could bring in the rest of the security team. First, I needed for him to leave the house and go somewhere to establish a routine. We were not going to get him anywhere near this Moonie house. That was too dangerous. My job from here was to wait and watch. Anyone leaving the house had to come out the front entrance. I had just finished my coffee and turned around to throw my cup in the trash. When I looked up, standing behind me was a really big man in a suit coat. He looked right in my eyes and opened his coat. What I saw next changed my day. Inside his jacket was an exceptionally large gun.

He kept his jacket open long enough to make sure I saw it. I was not the only person standing on the corner, but he was not interested in showing anyone else but me. I smiled turned around and started walking down the street. Without turning around, I knew he was walking behind me. I knew he meant business and I was his business. I was not going anywhere there were not a lot of people. I did not think he was dumb enough to use his gun with all these people walking around. But that did not matter now. He was still walking behind me. The small shops had already opened their doors and I turned and walked into one of them. He stopped right outside the door and just stood there. I figured if I stayed in there long enough, he would get bored and leave. I honestly believed the cult was going to move Teddy and this guy was brought in to make sure no one would follow them. It was either that or I had blown my cover. I will get back to that shortly.

After being there for some time and trying to keep one eye on the big man blocking my way out and the other eye on the Moonie house, he was still there. I started to get concerned and I was looking for another way out of the store. I found the rear entrance, but it was blocked from floor to ceiling with merchandise. I was not going out that door without making a commotion. I needed to come up with some way of moving the big man with his big gun away from the front of the store. But how? My mind went into overdrive and it did not take me long to come up with an idea. Now to see if it was going to work. I called the owner of the store over and told him the big man standing blocking his doorway had an exceptionally large gun in his jacket. I went on to tell him I knew he was not a policeman. He got right on the phone and called the police. Now all I had to do was wait. It took a little while, but it did bring the police to our location. When the big guy saw the police, car pull up he wasted no time getting out of there. I watched as he walked across the street and into the Moonie house. My first instinct was to get as far away from there as possible, but I could not. My job was not done yet. Whether or not my cover was blown did not matter now. What did matter was Teddy was still in the house, and I was not going to leave as long as he was still in there.

The Moonies knew who we were as a company. Now they knew about me. I was not going to be any good to Teddy or his parents, but I was not going anywhere unless they moved him from that house. Or until I could get a replacement in. I walked up the street to my car and placed a call to C and told him what just happened. C told me that someone would be there in two hours to replace me. I really did not want to be there when it got dark.

I went back over everything in my mind that happened over the last couple of days. I could not be sure if I had blown my cover or not. It happened so fast I do not believe the cult had time to put it all together. The big guy with the big gun was not the same guy that was at the top of the steps when I was leaving dinner. Teddy's bodyguards did not react when I pretended to be talking on my radio walking down the stairs. They would not have known Teddy as Teddy. They would have known him by his cult given name. The cult gives their new members new names when they join. I honestly believe they were being careful when it came right down to it with that much money at stake. Either way they knew about me now, and I could not be any more help to anyone. My replacement had arrived, and I felt good knowing Teddy would be in good hands. I was sent onto another case, but I was kept informed on Teddy's progress. I am happy to say the other group C brought in was successful in getting Teddy away from the cult and they did it in time to save the two million dollars that was at stake. I never heard how they did it, but it is my belief they were able to outsmart and overpower the Moonie security staff. At this point it did not matter.

Teddy was deprogrammed successfully and is doing well. For the cult they lost big time. As for the parents, I did not get the chance to see them again, but I did hear they were grateful for what we were able to achieve. I did not get to finish what I started, but I am glad to have been part of making it happen. All we can expect from ourselves is to do our best. That is all we have control over. All I have ever wanted was for these kids to have a fair shake in life, and removing them from these cults, gives them a fighting chance. My thanks go out to all the individuals that made this case have a happy ending. You know who you are. For myself, I left with the satisfaction in knowing Teddy was going to be ok. And that was enough for me. I continued with my work for as long as I could, and I will continue to write about these stories.

CHAPTER TEN

MOONIE CULT: SID

This story takes me to Nashville Tennessee. I got a call from C and he asked if I could help on a Moonie case. I liked removing these young kids from Moons cult. It was always fun to see what we would get into next. I am going to call this young man Sid. Sid had gotten caught up with the Moonies the same old usual way in California. After he went through Moons brainwashing, he was sent out on the streets to make Moon a lot of money, along with Moons thirty thousand other members that were under Moons control. He was sent to Nashville in the attempt to put him in a place his parents would not look for him.

We had deprogrammed a young girl awhile back that had also gotten caught up in Moons web. Her name is Marsha. Marsha had been working with our deprogramming teams for the past year and she had become a valuable asset to our company. She was in the office when Sid's folder came in the mail. After C opened the folder, he asked Marsha if she was ready to go on another Moonie case and she said sure. C handed the folder to her and when she opened it, she said she knew Sid. Thank goodness for miracles.

Up to now we did not know were Sid was. Neither did his parents. All they knew was he had gotten caught up in this religious group in San Francisco. Marsha had met Sid at the farm and worked with him in San Francisco. Sid's parents had taken things into their own hands and started making inquiries into their son's whereabouts. The problem was they had done it at the Moonie house where all the new recruits go to dinner. It did not take long before the cult sent him to another state. Sid's parents did not know how lucky they were Moon did not send Sid off to another country instead of another state.

Marsha and Sid had worked together long enough to become friends. Sid had mentioned to Marsha that his cult leader told him to pack his bags, he was being moved to another state. Sid did not know which state, but he did tell her he had overheard his leader talking about Nashville. That was all C needed to hear. C sent one security guy to Nashville to see if he could come up with Sid's whereabouts. Ted was that guy. Ted had been on enough cases he knew what he was doing. If Sid were in Nashville, he would find him. It was only a matter of time. Ted had been searching for Sid for two weeks without having any luck. He decided to check on another location the Moonies use to hang around. Before he was ready for that he needed to get some supplies. Ted parked his car and walked up to the front of the store, and there a few feet away stood Sid. Yes, sometimes it happens that way. He had gotten lucky. As a group we have always said we would rather be lucky than good.

To Sid, Ted was just another shopper. Ted should not have any problems watching Sid as long as he was careful. Sid continued to work the shopping center for the next few days and that would give C enough time to send in the troops. I was farther away from Ted, so I was going to be the last one to arrive. C and another security guy I had worked with on many occasions picked me up at the airport. C had booked us in a genuinely nice motel in Nashville. We arrived at the motel and pulled into a parking lot. We had walked about halfway to the entrance of the building and C threw me the car keys and asked if I would go back and get his briefcase. I said sure. They continued to walk the rest of the way to the lobby. I walked back to where the car was parked. It was not there. I looked everywhere and no car.

After looking around for five minutes I gave up. I walked back to the motel and just as I got to the door, I heard laughter. When I looked up there was the whole team standing on the balcony laughing their asses off at me. What I did not know was C had given one of the other securities guys the spare car key and he moved the rental car to the far side of the parking lot. There I was walking around the parking lot at a big motel looking for a rental car. The joke was on me. Believe me that little prank set the tone of humor I would carry with me the whole case. I went upstairs where everyone was waiting for me. They were waiting to start our meeting on what we were going to do next. Ted had done a good job in setting up a plan on how he wanted to remove Sid from this evil cult. We all agreed as usual. We were set up for the next day. If Sid kept to his same routine things should go well. One of the many things that C told me was when it comes to doing this kind of work do not over think it. I have always been the type of person that puts all of himself into his work. I always take this work personally. I hated the idea that these cults could control these young kids minds at will. I want to remove as many of these kids away from these so-called Messiah. Yes, I was over thinking my job. I never want to lose my edge or my drive. As our meeting concluded, I could tell there were a few guys that were still thinking about me walking around the parking lot looking for our rental car. Occasionally, someone would just start laughing and then everyone would join in. I was the cause of their laughter and I could not help it, I had to join in. Our meeting was over, and everyone knew what needed to be done. Tomorrow should be a piece of cake. Hopefully without any problems. Everyone went to the lounge to have dinner and drinks, but I decided to stay behind. I wanted to be fresh for the next day.

It was twelve o'clock when they came back from dinner. None of them were going to have a problem falling asleep. They had consumed enough alcohol to sleep like a baby. And for me I guess I was over thinking about tomorrow and I was wide awake. Before I knew it was five o'clock in the morning and I had not fallen asleep yet. It did not make any sense to try to sleep now. Not that I could have anyway. After a hot shower and three cups of coffee, I found myself walking around the parking lot and I probably would still be there if C would not have said it was time to get ready to go. I went upstairs to my room and my roommate had the tv on. There was a bank robbery going on two miles down the road. There were cops everywhere out looking for them. We could hear police sirens off in the distance and they were getting louder. I checked with the rest of the team and it was a go. Too much time had been spent finding Sid. We were not going to let anything stand in our way. All we could do was cross our fingers. We did not have extremely far to go and when we pulled in the parking lot, Sid and his teammates had just gotten out of their van. What happened next is what we were hoping for. Both cult kids were walking in different directions in the parking lot and it was time to make our move. Two of our security guys had already gotten into position and they were signaling for me to make my move. I drove through the parking lot and stopped my car right beside Sid and my teammates. Within seconds Sid was in the back seat of my car and we were pulling out of the lot.

We had driven for about thirty minutes and the farther we got away from the city the less we could hear the sirens. That made me happy. I kept looking in my rear-view mirror for my back up car and they were not behind me. I was going to need them soon, and I started to get concerned. It had been raining for the last week, but it was not raining now. Some of the roads were flooded and some were impassable. My next move was going to require me to get on the other side of the highway where our safe location was set up. In order to do that I had to make a left-hand turn, go under an overpass, turn again and our safe location was one mile down the road. The road we were on was drivable, but the water was getting deeper. The car in front of me made the left turn that I needed to do. The water was so deep his car stalled, and he could not get it started. Before I made my turn, I looked in my rear-view mirror again and there was my back up car. Thank goodness. If I ever needed him, now is the time. It was my turn to attempt to make the turn. It was going to be a long shot, but I could not go straight, and I did not want to head back in the same direction I just came from. I could almost see the building we were going to be staying in, but was I going to get there? I was glad to have my back up car behind me in case I got stuck. A least he could try to push me through the intersection. The little car in front of me was partly blocking the road and he was not going anywhere. I pulled forward trying to stay to the high side of the road. Just as I was making my last turn what I saw next shocked me. There was not anything I could do. I had to keep up my speed and go through the stop sign without stopping. What I saw when we made the last turn was the local news crew had their cameras set up on the side of the road and they were filming. Cameras rolling. Yep there was little doubt we made it on local television. I continued to drive out of the water and down the road to our safe house. When I looked in my mirror my back up car was on my tail. We pulled into our safe place and escorted Sid into the room we had set up for him. Once we got him settled in his room, I went into the living room and turned on the television set. I needed to see if we had made it on the news. As soon as I turned on the tv there we were. Not only did they get us on tape, they got my plate number along with a clear picture of myself. I looked like someone that did not want to be seen on the news. Along with that they captured Sid in the back seat trying to get their attention. It showed the security guys attempting to keep his arms pinned down. And to make things worst they got the backup cars plate number. After seeing this I told C and he agreed that we needed to find somewhere else to do this deprogramming. It was going to be dangerous traveling on the highway with these same two cars. We had no choice. We packed everything back up and loaded Sid back in the car and headed out. We were not going back the same way we came in, but it was the direction we needed to go. I needed to find another way around safely. We were back on the highway and Sid was behaving himself. We drove for some time without any problems. C informed me he put together another safe house. The problem was it was a ten-hour drive. If you remember I did not sleep last night because I was over thinking it. Now I was driving again, and it was going to be a long haul. I was concerned that Sid was going to act out during our long drive. By the time we reached our location, I was beyond tired.

When we pulled in the driveway the scenery was beautiful. We were snuggled in the mountains and the yard was manicured beautifully. Sid started to get a little cranky, but who could blame him. Things did not go as planned. When we were escorting him into the house, he let out a yell. His voice echoed through the mountains. Our security wasted no time in whisking him into the house. He was escorted to his room where he spent the next three weeks. I was so tired, but I was too pumped up to sleep. I decided to take the third shift, so I did not have to force myself to sleep. I had some time on my hands, so I went outside to check on one of our teammates. He suffered from allergies and he was not getting any better. He went outside so he would not disturb anyone. When I turned the corner of the house, I could hear him sneezing. I walked up to him and he sneezed so hard his denture flew out of his mouth and hit the only rock in the yard. It shattered the whole plate. Here we were a thousand miles away from home and he had no way to chew. He was going to have a hard time eating for the next few weeks. I went in and checked on Sid before going to sleep. He was doing as good as expected. Sid was not a negative person and it helped in his deprogramming. A couple of weeks had gone by since we arrived, and Sid was doing well. He had adjusted to his new surroundings and he was asking a lot of questions. The deprogrammers asked if we could take him for a walk in the mountains. It seemed to me that he had been deprogrammed successfully but it was not up to me to me to make that call. The deprogrammers had that say. I felt they were right. I told them it sounds fun. I decided to have a talk with Bill. He was the owner of the house we were staying in. He was familiar with the area. I asked him if he would join us and he said sure. I got back with the deprogrammers and set it up for the next day. I went into Sid's room and asked him if he wanted to come along. You should have seen the look on his face. He had not been outside since we picked him up. Bill had told me to expect a few hikers along the way. He also said this was the off season so the foot traffic should be light. The next morning Sid was sitting with his shoes on before anyone was up, He was ready. Both of his parents came along with two deprogrammers, three security guys and Bill. We had been out for about two hours and everything was going well. To me it seemed there were a lot more hikers on the trails than was expected. We stayed out on the trails for about another hour before heading back to the house. Sid enjoyed the day and he asked if it was possible to go back one more time before we leave. I made travel arrangements for the end of the week. As for the security guy with his sneezing and his broken plate, he got by with eating soft foods and he did not complain once. As for Sid, he went through rehab with his parents and is at home an doing well. As for the bank robbers in Nashville they got caught. This is a happy ending for Sid and his family. Other than the ten-hour drive to our safe house things could not have gone any better. Sid is happy, his parents are happy. And the Moonies lost another one to the good guys. The reason for all the people on the trails, Bigfoot had been spotted in the area. Go figure.

CHAPTER ELEVEN

DEVINE LIGHT MISSION CULT: DENISE

After getting the call from my boss C, I was sent on my first DLM case. It was a walk in. The name of the group was Devine Light Mission or for short DLM. DLM was founded by a guru by the name of Shri Hans Maharaja from northern India. At that time, the DLM had over a million members. Shri died in 1966 and his predecessor was Prem Rewwat who was eight years old at the time of Shri's death. By the time Prem was sixteen years old he had taken control of the Western States. Prem was a powerful force. But he was just another False Prophet. His sole purpose was to manipulate his followers in believing he was the true Messiah. All his members are required to give up all their worldly possessions. They are also required to denounce their family members. His followers have been known to turn over millions of dollars to the group just to prove their loyalty. This is where we come in.

The name of this cult kid I will call Denise. Our group was hired by Denise's mother, who I will call Betty. We were being asked to help out if we could. What was required of our security personnel on this case was to show up a couple of hours before Denise would be coming home. We did what was called a walk in. It did not require any surveillance or a pickup. Betty told us Denise would be coming home around one o'clock on Friday. What we needed to do was to make sure Denise did not try to leave her home once she arrived. Part of my job is also security. C had already sent three security guys along with one deprogrammer to Bettys home and they were waiting for Denise to arrive. They did the usual job securing Bettys home for everyone's safety. This is done by removing any objects that could be used as a weapon, and also securing the home. Denise had pulled her car into the driveway and was getting her bags from her car. She entered the house, put her things down on the table and walked into the kitchen. Our security staff stepped in front of her and she was not happy. They explained they were here to have a talk with her. She decided she did not want any part of this and tried to go out the door. She was stopped by one security guy standing by the door. He told her to sit down and behave herself. Denise decided to get violent and started swinging her arms in the attempt to harm someone. She was quickly restrained and set down on the couch. After a few bad words she directed towards her mother, she calmed down. I arrived shortly after this happened. I was brought in to replace one of our security people that was needed elsewhere.

Denise was a very bright musician who cut a couple albums with her band before she got caught up in the cult.

On the way over to Bettys home I was informed Denise had been shopping and she was driving her own car doing errands. This struck me funny because everything I knew about this cult, no one was ever allowed to go anywhere by themselves. They would not have any reason to do any shopping. And why was she driving her own car? These things were not allowed in this cult. Things were not adding up. And I just arrived. I would later find out why. I arrived at Bettys home and Denise was sitting on the couch. I went over and sat down across from Denise and I introduced myself. This would be my first time dealing with this cult. I had some training but not much. C had told me to keep my emotions in check. I would find out later how hard that would be. I do have to say I was a little nervous, and I really did not know what to expect. Time would tell. I was told that the house was secured before my arrival. But as good as our team is, sometimes things are overlooked.

I just sat down and did not realize Denise was drinking from a glass. I should have picked up on it right away, but I did not. Before I could remove the glass from her hand, she slammed it down on the table and broke it. She decided she was going to make a statement. Before I knew what was happening, Denise leaned over the table, and cut me with the glass. I had just bought these jeans the day before. I wanted to look presentable. The glass cut into my leg and it was bleeding through my pants. Even though I was bleeding I was still able to remove the glass from her hand before she could do any more harm to anyone else or herself. I soon learned she had full control of her emotions and she would turn them on and off at will. To me that did not make any sense for someone under mind control.

I took the time to bandage myself up. The security team had moved Denise to her bedroom where she would remain. The deprogrammers had been talking with her and she did calm down somewhat. Like many of you I was skeptical that mind control was even real. As I was about to find out it is very real. As the years went on, I was to learn how much damage mind control can cause. I can attest to its validity and to the harm it brings to these young adults and their families. Mind control is used by these religious cults to relinquish power, and to indoctrinate their followers into doing their will. While I was tending to my wound the other security members took care of the glass and made sure she was given plastic everything. No knives of any kind. That made me happy. I made sure everything was accounted for after every meal. Mistakes happen. I was glad she did not think about hurting herself. I could see we all had a few things to learn. I only blame myself for the hole in my leg.

She stayed pretty calm the rest of the time we spent with her, and that bothered me. She had a lot of anger built up inside and I was sure she would act out again. But she did not. We spent the next ten days with Denise and her mother. The deprogrammer concluded that Denise's situation was much worse than we had anticipated. Her mother finally told us she had been kicked out of the cult after she had given them all of her savings. She was no longer any use to the cult. It was bad enough she felt like she no longer fit into normal society, now she been rejected by the cult. She had come to believe that Prem was her true Messiah. It was too much for her to accept. We could see she had deep rooted problems, and we were not going to be able to help her. She needed a different type of professional care. Our deprogrammer had contacted the office and explained the situation. They all agreed what needed to be done. He sat down with Betty and explained what could be done to help Denise. The next day our office put Betty in touch with someone that was used to dealing with these types of situations. After a couple of months, I was informed about Denise's progress, and I am happy to say she is back to making music. Denise was brainwashed into believing the cult life was the only life to live. The experience I had with her and her mother proved to be heart wrenching. It drove me to learn everything I could about these religious cults and what it really means to be brainwashed. What I hope to portray through these stories is just how powerful mind control is, and the damage it causes both physically and mentally. Mind control cannot be taken lightly. Our job as parents never ends. Everyone is someone's child. I would spend a few more years working with the deprogrammers to remove as many of these young adults from these religious cults. Unfortunately, not all of them have happy endings.

CHAPTER TWELVE

MOONIE CULT: MARK

I had just finished up on a case in Arizona and I wanted to check up with some of my coworkers that were working on a case in San Francisco. Our leader that was running this case I will call Stan. Stan was sent to San Francisco to find a young man I will call Mark. Mark was not your typical Moonie. He had attempted to pass the bar exam once before he arrived in San Francisco. He had been in the city just a few weeks. He was sightseeing like a lot of people do and that is when he ended up at Fisherman's Wharf. That is where he was approached by one of Moons recruiters. It did not take long for him to get caught up in what the cult was offering him. They promised him the world. Moon had plans for Mark. He was not with the Moonies exceptionally long and he was sent back to take the bar exam. Moons plans were to make Mark a congressman. Moon had a lot of connections in Washington. He gave millions of dollars to some of our elected officials over time. Moon was taking real good care of Mark.

He had someone to drive him around, and he was kept separate from the other cult members. He was given room and board and spending money. He thought he had it all. Moon was not going to give up on Mark because of how valuable he was to Moons plans. Mark was very smart but not when it came to street smarts. It is hard for Moons recruiters to recruit young kids that have been brought up to know what it is like to struggle from time to time. Most of the kids he goes after are the middle to upper class kids. The richer the better. Stan had already located Mark and he knew right where he was going to make the pickup. When I flew in after checking with Stan, I asked if he had enough help for what he was about to do, and he told me yes. I was told the pick-up was going to be done right in the middle of San Francisco, in the middle of the day. There were going to be hundreds if not thousands of people hanging around. After hearing that I had to see it for myself. One thing about Stan, nothing ever bothered him. It did not Matter what it was. He is one of the bravest individuals I have ever known. We decided to have a quick lunch and then walk to the site were Stan and his crew were going to attempt to remove Mark from this cult. Stan and I had finished eating first so we went outside to wait for the rest of his crew to get done. We walked across the street just about the time the other guys finished eating and they were coming out of the restaurant. Stan had instructed them to walk up the other side of the street so we would not be seen all together. We were one day away from the pickup and they needed to be careful. Back in those days any more than three people walking in a group was considered a gang. As we walked past an alley a man walked up behind us and wanted to start a fight. You could tell he had been beat up before and it was not that long ago. His face and hands still had blood on them as did his clothes. At first, we just laughed. There was one of him and two of us. He would not have stood a chance. He was beat up to start with. He kept on being persistent. We just kept on walking and had traveled two blocks when out from another alley walked four of his friends. One of them pulled out a big knife and was threatening to stab us if we did not do what he wanted. Both of us started to laugh again and that made these dudes even madder. Now it was five against two. They thought they had the odds in their favor, but they were about to find out different. Once our other guys saw what was going on, they started walking across the street. Stan was over six feet tall and two of his teammates made him look little. Both were ex-football players. As soon as these thugs got a glimpse of what was about to happen, they ran away like little puppies. One of them was still waving that big knife as he ran past his friends. Yes, it was funny. I learned a lesson that afternoon. If you are ever going to go downtown San Francisco for lunch take some big friends with you. Remember this was forty years ago.

It did not take us long to reach the pickup area. Stan was planning to grab Mark as he came out of the office building where he was taking his bar exam. What they were about to do was crazy. Not only did they have to get him into their car, but they had to do it with hundreds of people hanging around. And if that was not crazy enough it was going to be done in the middle of the day. There were always people sitting around eating lunch, and people walking in and out of different buildings. And to make things even worse there were police walking and riding bikes everywhere. Add in the fact there were also venders with their food carts.

Well, I had seen enough. We headed back to our motel rooms and waited for the next day to arrive. This is one case I was glad I was not helping with. The chance of making this work was exceedingly small. They just had too many things going against them. The next day came as it usually does, and I really believed that I was going to be the one that bails them all out of jail. It was time and Stan's crew were ready. Mark should be walking out the front door from taking his exam. One thing Stan had going for them was Mark may have a lot on his mind after taking his exam. He might be a little distracted. That would help. Mark came out of the building and headed for the corner of the street. I knew he would have his cult leader waiting for him somewhere, but where? Mark was leaning up against a pole that had the crosswalk sign on it. As soon as Stan's crew started to grab Mark, he grabbed the pole with both hands and would not let go. The getaway car was already in place with the back door open. His security team had ahold of both of his legs, and he is stretched straight out. They were able to get his hands free from the pole and he was being escorted into the back of the getaway car. It was not over by any means. They still had to get out of the city before there was any light at the end of the tunnel. One thing about being in this city you are required to stop for anyone walking in the street regardless if they do not have the right of way. It is the law. Block by block they creeped along as Mark was trying to get his hands free so he could draw attention to himself. If no one came to his rescue when he was stretched out from the pole, I do not believe anyone would interfere now. Remember this is San Francisco. Everyone at that time was out for themselves. Not much of a chance of anyone interfering now. Even if someone would try, Stan's back up car was right behind them ready to jump in at any time.

They had six blocks to get out of downtown before they would hit the highway. After Mark saw his father's face he calmed down. It was a two-hour drive to their safe house, and he remained calm. He gave security no problems when he was taken into the safe house.

Stan's team had done it. They pulled off the impossible. I could not believe it. Everything was against them and they got it done. My hats off to all of them. It is totally amazing what can be done when you put your mind to it and believe in your team.

Mark was happy being in the Moonies. He was going to do what he dreamt of doing and someone was going to pay for it. As far as he was concerned, he thought he had it made. What he did not know was he would be under the watch of the cult for the rest of his life, whatever kind of life that would be. Hopefully, the deprogrammers will be able to get him to see what the cult was all about. It was not going to be easy. He was treated differently because of how smart he was, and what he could do for the cult. One of the good things that the deprogrammers had going for them was Mark was a Christian and he did study his bible. This would be helpful in deprogramming him. He was familiar with the Christian way. All these religious cults change the wording around and remove whole sentences in the bible to twist things around to fit Moon teachings. Moon believed he was the way to eternal life and his followers believe in him. He is nothing but a false prophet who is driven by greed and backed or guided in part by the Korean government.

It did not take long for Mark to see right through Moons theories and his teachings. All he needed was someone to show him the truth. He was helped by the deprogrammers and they would stay with him as long as he needed them. It took about two weeks for him to see the truth and then he was taken to our rehab center where he got more help. He was happy to find out that he passed the bar exam. After spending time at rehab, he went on to be one of the best deprogrammers we had working with us. It was his goal to help remove as many cult kids from Moons grasp. He stayed working with us for the next couple years. He did go on to become a successful attorney and he is doing well. As far as the cult was concerned, they lost one more to the good guys. That makes me happy. I did not work on this case, but I felt I needed to write about it. Stan's teamed pulled off the impossible. Their devotion and courage never fail to amaze me.

CHAPTER THIRTEEN

MOONIE CULT: BOBBIE

This story is about a very pretty young woman I will call Bobbie. Bobbie was in her early twenties when she got caught up in the Moonies. That was four years ago. My first objective was to find her. I was told she could be in New York. That is where I will start. I had worked there many times before and I knew of a couple of Post Office boxes the cult had used in the past. After flying out the next day and grabbing a rental car, I headed for the closest P O box. Bobbie's job was to solicit flowers and trinkets on the streets. She would not be doing this alone. I was sure I would find her with a group of ten cult kids. There is a difference between Moons regular soliciting teams and what Bobbie was doing. She was working with Moons mobile fund-raising teams. These teams would have ten members that would travel across the United States soliciting Moons goods. They could spend weeks at a time just going from one town to another. This makes finding her and removing her from the cult that much harder, because they do not stay in one spot long.

Following a mobile fund-raising group for any length of time becomes more difficult and it is hard not to be noticed. They would start out in the mornings by seven am and would not return until dark. Once they got their vans loaded, they would start their journey. It would not take very long before the driver of their van would do what is called a flip flop. As they are driving in one direction without any notice they would turn around in the middle of the street and would be heading in the other direction. We never knew when they would do this or how many times. It all depended on how far they were going to travel that day. If the location they picked out for that day was not far from their home, we could expect them to start flip flopping right way. What the driver is doing is to give these kids enough time to psyche themselves up enough before hitting the streets with Moons trinkets and crap. If the distance were farther away from home, they would do their chanting on the drive. Either way we just do not know where they are heading until they get there.

I had spent two days staking out the first post office box and on the third day a Moonie van pulled in and retrieved their mail. You ask how did I know it is a Moonie van? That is a good question. It is hard to tell right off the bat until the driver gets out of their van. All of Moons male cult kids have shaved heads and a ponytail. It is hard to miss them. Most of these Moonie vans have tinted windows. But not all of them. After he retrieved their mail, he was heading out of the parking lot and going in the same direction he just came from. He drove around doing errands for a little while before he led me right to his house. Now was the waiting game. I was going to stay parked up the street from this house until I was sure Bobbie was or was not living there. As far as I knew she could be hundreds or thousands of miles away. I just did not know.

I sat and waited until dark when the first police car showed up. I had been expecting him for some time now. I was in a neighborhood watch area and it did not take long for someone to report me. With my window down and my arm sticking out the window this policeman should feel more comfortable knowing it is a little safer to approach my car. I needed to stay on the right side of the law for as long as it took to do my job. I was not going to be any good to anyone sitting at the police station, or in the back of his squad car. I needed to keep a low profile. The officer took my badge and then he called my office to check up on me. When he was done, he handed me back my badge and said do not do anything to break the law and then he walked off. There were so many cults around at that time and these police officers knew about them. Most of the officers I met really do not care for them. Or should I say they did not like what was happening to these young kids. It was their leaders they did not like. He knew why I was here. I just need to be careful. I figured I had been here long enough. If this were the house, she was staying in, I figured I would be following them around for some time. I could not do anymore tonight, so I headed for a motel.

My plan for the next day was to return and wait for the post man to show up. I did not believe what I was going to do would work but I had to try. It was ten o'clock before I arrived, but it was just in time for the post woman. I showed her my badge along with a picture of Bobbie and asked her if she knew who lived in that house. She looked at me and said she did not deliver mail to that house and even if she did, she could not tell me who lived there. I thanked her and she went on her way. The same van I followed here yesterday was still parked in the driveway. I sat there for an hour and no one came in or out of the house. I headed back to my room. I waited until almost dark and I headed back to this house. When I got there, there was another van in the driveway. There was an alley that ran behind this Moonie house, so I drove in and parked one house away. I tried to get close enough to see in their windows, but the curtains were pulled shut. I knew everyone was in the front of the house because I could hear them chanting. They chanted a lot and before meals was one of those times.

I snuck up behind their house and removed their trash from the trash can. I got back in my car and went back to my room where I dumped their trash into my bathtub. I had done this before only to find out that the cult had gotten smarter and shredded their trash. It was worth a try. Bingo I got lucky. There was a list of all the names of everyone that was living in this house. It also gave the amounts of how much money had been taken in that week. Bobbies name was on that list. These kids were averaging five hundred dollars a day each. This was a household full of experienced kids. This was not going to be easy.

Well now I had located her at least on paper, which made me happy. My next step was to return tomorrow early enough to see Bobbie get into which van. I could not take the chance of the police showing up again, especially at night. I waited until dinner was over before I went back to my motel. By the sound of the chanting they were doing I did not believe there were more than ten kids in the house having dinner. So, what was the other van for? Was it going to leave tonight? And if so, would Bobbie be in it? I did not think so because there were only ten names on the list I had, and Bobbies name was one of them. I believed this other van was being used by a couple of cult leaders probably picking up all the cash these kids took in. When I arrived the next day, I was too late to see who got loaded in what van. They were already pulling out of the driveway. I almost missed them. I was late getting here this morning I needed to pick up some supplies I would need, especially if they decided to make a long haul. I needed to be prepared. When these kids go mobile fund raising, I cannot just stop what I am doing and run off to get what I need. It could be hours before they might stop for the night and if they had two drivers available, they may never stop. I had been caught with my pants down before as they say, and I was not going to go through that again. It is a tough job following a mobile fund-raising group for any length of time without blowing your cover. I was hoping it would not come to that but if it did, I was ready.

They made the decision to solicit local today, so after watching them do three flip flops, and me trying not to be seen they finally ended up at a shopping center. The driver of the van only dropped off two kids and drove off. I followed. After two more stops and dropping of his kids we were at the end of the line and the last of the kids had been dropped off but no Bobbie. I decided to head back to my room, but before doing so I went back by their house. I waited for a while and no one came in or out of the house. Back to my room I went. I would make sure I was there earlier the next day.

The next day came too early but I was sitting watching as everyone in this house loaded into this one van. And yes, Bobbie was one of them. I counted ten kids. That is the right amount for a mobile fund-raising trip. Were we in for a long drive? Only time would tell. Now I had found Bobbie and this time in the flesh and for that I was proud. I was happy I did not have to spend weeks on the road not knowing if I was in the right state looking for her. Sometimes this job is a crap shoot. I guess that is what makes it so much fun. Well my job had just begun. When I found the time, I would let my office know I found her so they could get everyone ready. I still did not know if we were going local or for a road trip. This Moonie house did not have a garage, so I was not able to see if they had any camping gear with them or not. I was hoping they did not.

Ok now we were driving down the road in the same direction they took yesterday, and I was waiting for them to flip flop. The driver of the van did not disappoint me. He was in his second time flip flopping and I was worried that this time I would not find a place to get out of their sight. It had been raining for a couple of days and the roads were wet. The drain sewers were not keeping up with the rain fall. This really limited my places to go. There was a construction site on my right and just before they drove by me, I whipped into the entrance of this site and was not expecting what happened next. The area was flooded and when my car hit the water hole it spun me around and I ended with the rear of the car backed into a mud pile. My car stalled as the mud got shoved up the exhaust pipes and everything just stopped. The water was deep but not too deep for me to get out and clear the mud loose from my exhaust pipes. I finally got my car started and I was standing there soaking wet. I pulled out of the site and started my search all over again. Too much time had passed. I had lost them. I decided to keep this little mishap to myself. I did not want to tell anyone that I had found and lost her in one day. I was hoping this was just another day trip and not a trip out of the area. All I could do at this time was go check into another room and dry out. I had a hunch this day was going to be a long one, so I had checked out of my motel just in case. I returned to their house early the next day but this time I decided it was too much of a risk to park up the street. So, I picked a spot around the corner to park. I was hoping they would drive out the same way they had done the last two days. If so, they should drive right past me. Shortly after I parked, their van drove past me. I still did not know if Bobbie was in the van or not. The windows had too much tint on them to get a good look. The van I had been following had the right rear taillight broken and it was put back together with duct tape. It was not going to be too hard to follow if they decided to travel a far distance. Up to now I have been forced to follow them at a close distance and I was not comfortable doing that. If we hit the highway the duct tape should stand out and I can fall back and still keep an eye on them. We had been driving for about one hour and they had not flip flopped one time. I found out later why. They turned onto the turnpike and I followed. After driving from a safe distance, we came to our first toll booth. I got behind a semi for some cover and by the time we made it through the booth their van was out of site. A few hundred yards ahead the road went up a small hill and then started going downhill. What I saw next was too much. Besides the state highway patrol sitting on the side of the road, the road went in three different directions. Which one did they take? After getting around the police car I pulled over to the side of the road. I got out of my car and stood on the hood hoping to find some sign of that taillight. A few seconds later a van the same color drove around a bend then he was out of sight. I had no other option than to follow. It took some time to catch up to the van, and when I got close enough to see, the right rear taillight had been taped up. I stayed back a distance keeping an eye on that taillight. After following them for a while I got this funny feeling in my gut something was wrong. I was happy I caught up to them again. But did I? That feeling did not go away. What was causing that feeling? I caught up to the van and my heart dropped. Yes, it was the same color van and it did have the right rear taillight taped up, but and there is that but. It did not have tinted windows. How could I have missed that? I had lost them again. Boy did I feel bad. What were the chances of two vans the same color and both had a broken right rear taillight? No matter what I told myself it did not change things. Bobbie and her crew could be in another state in a few hours. But which one? I had enough for the day, and I was feeling dumb. I had been doing this work for some time now and I genuinely believed I was rather good at my job. It did not matter what I thought, the facts are the facts and this fact was, I had lost them twice and for that I vowed to never let it happen again. I was more pumped up now to find her and get her away from this cult. I went and checked into a motel close to their house hoping they were on a short distance trip and they would be returning home soon. What I did not know was things were going to get worse.

I returned to their house for the next four days and nights and no Moonie vans. This way of thinking was not getting me anywhere, so it was time for another strategy. I checked out of my room the next day and decided to go by the house one more time. After not seeing any vans in the driveway I drove back to the post office box. I had not parked for two minutes and another Moonie van pulled into the post office. He retrieved their mail and was pulling out of the parking lot. It was not the same van Bobbie was in, but it was a Moonie van. I followed. He had not driven very far, and he was pulling into his driveway. This was not the same van nor was this the same Moonie house. Around the back of the house was the van with the broken right rear taillight. I got lucky. I had found them again. The amount of joy I felt was unexplainable. I had thought I had lost my chance to help Bobbie, but I never gave up. One day I felt terrible and a few days later I am back in the game. I waited for some time to see if anything was going to change. It was calm with little movement, so I returned to the motel I was staying in only to find out they were booked and were going to stay that way for another week. I tried a couple other motels in the area, but they were also booked. I drove over to the next town and checked there. I really did not want to get too far away from this new Moonie house, but I needed a place to sleep.

When I arrived it was getting dark? The town I was in was too small to have any lodging. On the one corner was an ice cream shop, so I pulled in to get some directions. I got out of my car and started walking towards the window. I heard a loud voice coming from across the street. It said hey let us go over and turn that little car upside down. I could tell I was in redneck heaven. I knew they were talking about me because I was the only one in the parking lot. I turned around and walked back to my car. I did not know if they were kidding or not. I soon found out. Just as I started my car and started to pullout two of the four rednecks were flying off my fenders. I knew when they hit the ground they were in pain. They were running fast towards me and I was picking up speed when we collided. The parking lot was gravel and that had to add to their pain. Now I knew these guys meant business and somehow, I became their business. By this time there was little doubt they were serious. I did not need to look back. As soon as they could get back to their trucks they would be after me. They knew their way around and I did not. It was dark and any street I would turn on could be a dead end. I was heading out of town not knowing where I was going. When I looked in my rear-view mirror, I saw head lights coming out of the bar those red necks came from. I could hear the rocks hitting the other cars in the parking lot. Their truck was throwing rocks everywhere and on everything nearby. There was going to be a few people ticked off when they came out of the bar and saw all the gravel on their trucks. There was no doubt they were after me. I was far enough ahead of them and I pulled into someone's driveway. I did not stop there. I drove across their lawn and around their garage before I stopped. Within seconds the rednecks flew past me and a few seconds later they were out of site. I did not know what was going to be worse, shot by these folks that lived in this house, or the rednecks out chasing me. I did not waste any time getting the heck out of there. I ended up getting back on the road but do not ask me how. I did not drive out the same way I drove in, fearing the homeowners were sitting on their porch with a shotgun waiting for me to drive by. I was heading back towards the center of town where those rednecks came from. As I drove by the bar what went through my mind was to go into the bar and sit down, grab a beer, and wait for those rednecks to give up and head back to this bar. The look on their faces would be priceless. I decided to keep on driving. I did not want to be buried alive in a shallow grave out in the middle of nowhere.

I needed to focus. I still needed to find a room. I was not going to worry about the speed limits. If I were to get pulled over at least I could get some directions. I was lost and tired. Any turn I made could lead me back to those rednecks. All I knew was they had to catch me first and so far, they were not smart enough.

I drove for some time before reaching a town that had a motel. I parked out front of the motel and went inside to get a room. When I walked in the woman behind the counter said they were all booked. She said the hotel down the street may have some vacancies. She got on the phone and checked for me. I was in luck. She had them hold the room for me. I thanked her and walked outside to my car. When I looked up it was gone. I could not believe what was happening to me. The first thing that went through my mind was those rednecks had found me, and they took my car. After thinking about it for a couple minutes I decided these rednecks would not just settle for getting my car, especially the two of them that flew off my car and landed on the gravel. I knew that hurt. They were out for blood. That was funny, four of them and one of me. If and when they find me, they were not going to settle for anything less than my hide. As I looked around, I saw my car at the end of the parking lot under a big pickup truck. I had to climb through the back window to pull it out from under this truck. It did not do any damage to his truck, but my car, that was a different thing. Other than the noise it made when I pulled out from under the truck, no one knew what had happen. It was late and everyone must have been asleep. It took some time to straighten my hood and pull my fender away from the tire. No one came out of their rooms, so I did not stick around. I did not want to lose the only room I had. I drove down the street to the other hotel and parked around the back. The only thing I could figure out was I must have had my car in neutral when I parked it and there was just enough of a slope for it to roll forward. At this point in time it did not matter. What I did not know, it was not over yet. I went into the hotel and checked in. I did not even take my bag in with me. All I wanted to do was sleep. I was happy to think I was in the clear and I was going to get some sleep. Things were looking up. Or were they? I got all the way down the hallway to the elevator when I heard someone yell out hold that door. I could hear someone running towards me, but I did not turn around. By the sound of it I believed it was only one person coming up behind me. The elevator door opened, and I stepped in. I did nothing to hold the door but whoever was behind me stepped in also. What I noticed was this dude had no bags. He did not reach over and push the button for his floor. At that time, I knew there was going to be a fight and I knew who was going to win. I had had enough, and I was not going to stop until I put this dude on his knees. The elevator stopped on my floor and I got off. Even though he was in front of me he stood there and waited for me to get off. I walked the ten feet to my room, and I never looked back. I knew he was behind me. I had my card ready to open my door. Having no bags my hands were free. I stuck my card in the slot and opened the door. The whole time he was standing behind me. He said nothing, nor did I. I stepped into my room and with the door still in my grasp, I gave it a shove as hard as I could, just as he stuck his foot in the doorway. When the door hit his ankle, I could hear bone break. When I turned around, he was laying on the hallway floor holding his ankle. He was in a lot of pain and I did not give a shit. Excuse my choice of words. I stood there and smiled. I said I was going to bring him to his knees. This was even better. I did not have to break a sweat to do it. I shut the door and called down to the front desk. I told them what happened, and they would need a stretcher. He was not going to go anywhere on his own. They told me he was not a guest of this hotel, and he has done this before. I assured them he will think twice before doing it again. They said they would send someone right away. Was it over for now? Yes. I was locked behind a closed door, tired, and I had been through all I could take for one day. It took me awhile to fall asleep. I just could not help thinking about those rednecks driving around still looking for me. That is funny. Well I would find out in the morning whether my car was where I parked it, but for now, sleep.

After a good night sleep, it was time to start again and head back to the house. It took me some time to get my thoughts together. I needed to put yesterday and last night out of my head. Maybe a nice drive in the country would do the trick. If I did not drive past sixty-five mph my car ran well. Any more speed than that it would start to shake. I do not think it liked being parked underneath a big pickup truck. Well I got lucky again. I got back in time to see Bobbie get into one of the vans and they drove off. I followed them to the other house, and everyone got out and went inside. A few minutes later she was back on the road with me behind them. They were heading for a college town. Boy I wished I knew about this town last night. The driver dropped all of them off at a stretch of stores. Bobbie was working with just one other person. This was a prime location and they were going to pull in a bundle of money. It was my belief they would be here all day and then return the next day to do it all over again. I felt good enough seeing this location I was not going to need to return to their house in the morning. I checked into a motel close by after checking at several motels until I found one that had a vacancy. The chances of getting a room in this college town last night would have been difficult. The reason the motels were full was because of the college playoffs. That explained that. I rested well and it was nice to have those few hours that I did not have to do anything or go anywhere. It was just before dark and the boredom had started to set in, so I jumped into my banged-up car and drove back over to their house. When I arrived, her van was sitting in the driveway. Also parked down the street was the same officer that had approached me earlier. I was not going to worry about him. He did not see me, and I felt if he did, he would not care. I sat there for a little while keeping one eye on the rear of the police car and one on the house. Just as I was about to leave, out walked Bobbie and two other cult kids.

They jumped into their van and drove off. I did not want to drive past the officer, but they just did. I took the chance and went around the block and I caught up to them at a traffic light. Again, I was lucky, they could have gone either way. They drove back to the same college town, but instead of going back to the same location they went into the bar district. I was confused but not for long. Their van pulled into the alley behind the bars and what I saw next I have never seen before. After parking their van one of her teammates got out of the front passenger's seat and walked to the side door of their van. Out popped Bobbie. No that is not what shocked me, it is what happened next. This same cult kid reached into the van and pulled out a wheelchair and opened it up. By this time, the driver had gotten out of the van and sat in the chair. Bobbie reached into the van and pulled out a couple boxes of flowers and handed them to the dude in the chair. The other guy got back into the van and laid down. If I was right, he was going to take a nap. Bobbie pushed the guy in the chair the short distance down the alley and into one of the bars. They stayed in there for some time.

They would go from bar to bar. When Bobbie would get low on flowers the other guy in the van would bring them to her. I still do not know how he knew to do that, but he did. I guess they had done this so many times it just came natural to them. I do not know how much money they racked in that night, but I am sure it was a bundle. One thing about college kids the more they drink the more generous they become. These Moonie kids are not allowed to keep any of this money. It all goes to Reverend Moon. All three of these kids have been working since seven a.m. and with a short break for dinner, they are back at it. It is now two o'clock in the morning. Long hours, no pay, no medical care. Sounds like brainwashing.

This was all I needed to see so I went back to my room and made the decision not to return to their house in the morning. I slept well and was back at it at ten o'clock the next morning. I headed for the shopping area and right there in the parking lot were the same three kids that were at the bar district until after two am. There was not any more I could do today, so I returned to my room and called for my teammates. Sara told me no one was available for a couple more days. I could not wait that long. I had been following this group for way to long now and it was only a matter of time before my luck would run out. Besides, Bobbie's routine can change at a moment's notice. The police could catch them for soliciting without a permit. They could be run out of town. I could not take that chance. I knew where our other team was working, and they were close by. The other team had two deprogrammers with them that worked security from time to time, along with the regular staff they always traveled with. I was going to call Sara and ask if I could steal some of them. They had been on their case for some time now, so they should be finishing up soon. We always like to have a short break between cases. If they did not have other plans, I know they would volunteer. Sara called back a few minutes later and said they were about to finish up with their case and they would be on their way. She said with any luck that should be the next day. I thanked her and hung up. Again, I was lucky. I figured I had two days at the most if the police did not interfere. Cross my fingers. I really did not want to start all over again. They showed up the next day and Bobbie's parents were a couple hours behind them.

After meeting with all of them we decided to take Bobbie at night at the bar district. It seemed to be the safest and we were all about safety. These cult kids were pulling in a lot of money for Moon and his cult leaders were not going to miss out on the opportunity to cash in. I was sure she would return.

It was Thursday and Bobbie worked the day shift, but no one worked the night shift. I was not surprised to see that. She would be back Friday night with her two teammates using their same scam. I went over with Bobbie's parents what their roll was going to be in this, and they said ok. They were nervous but ready. We were staying with our plan. Friday drug on forever but we were pumped up and ready to go. It was time for me to head for their house. It was close to dark when I arrived. I could see well enough only when the porch light would come on. Either someone was coming or going. The light was on a motion sensor in case someone was to walk up to the porch or pull in the driveway. All I needed to do was stay cool and wait for them to lead me to the bar district, where everyone was waiting patiently. Bobbie was right on time. The three of them were loading their van and shortly they would be pulling out of the driveway. Again, we were on our way. Everything was going as planned. Or was it? They did not make the right turn to get to the parking lot. What was going on? I was right behind them and a couple blocks down the road they did a flip flop. Now things were making sense. I was able to drive right past them because I had traded rental cars with one of my teammates. I decided to not drive past them again just in case they decided to flip flop again, which I expected them to do. I headed for the pickup spot. It was a gamble, but I was willing to take that chance. So far, they had not done anything I had not expected them to do. I knew they would be by soon. Bobbie's team picked this parking lot for a reason. It was dark and isolated. They did not want anyone to see them start their little scam with the wheelchair. This parking lot was perfect for them and us. We had checked out of our motel rooms and things were about to get exciting. When I arrived, everyone was in position and eager, except for her parents. Needless to say, they have never been in this type of situation before, and if I could sum it up correctly, they were scared shitless. They knew what to expect but it is not like being there. They did not want anything to go wrong, neither did we. We planned it as carefully as we could, but there is always the unknown. It took a half hour before her group showed up. But show up they did. I was relieved. Their driver parked in the same spot he had used in the past. There was little chance that anyone else was going to park close by. They were parked in a loading and unloading zone only. They must have known that there were not any deliveries at night. They all did exactly what they had done before with the exception that Bobbie grabbed more boxes of flowers than before. Everything was picture perfect. It was dark except for a security light at the far end of the lot. Here we go. Bobbie was pushing her teammate down the alley like before. This time two of our security guys were walking behind her and one was walking towards her. The guy in front had a twenty-dollar bill in his hand and he was waving it to get her attention. Once she got a look at that bill, she was so focused she did not realize our two security guys were standing behind her. When she saw the money in his hand she let go of the chair and took one step to grab it. That is when it all went down. By this time, I had already driven up next to them and I turned around and opened the back door. Before anyone knew what just happened, she was escorted into the back seat of my car and we were heading away from the bar district. What was funny was the security guy that had the bill in his hand sat down in the lap of the guy in the wheelchair and he did not do a thing to intervene. Seconds later our back up car had driven by and picked up the security guy sitting on top of the cult kid. As the security guy was getting up, he reached back and grabbed a few boxes of flowers and threw them in the car as they all drove off. I believe the cult kid in the wheelchair was so scared he did not know what to do, so he just sat there. I found out later while all of this was going on our back up car driver let the air out of one of the tires as the other cult kid was laying down trying to take his nap. He did this just in case he got wind of what was going on and decide to follow us. It worked better than I had expected, and the parents were also surprised and relieved.

I went through my normal routine and told Bobbie we were here to talk with her. She said nothing. I went on to say she needed to stay calm and no one would lay a hand on her. Again, she was quiet. With her mother in the front seat, it helped keep her calm knowing she was not going to be harmed. She remained calm all the way to our safe house and that concerned me. She was holding back a lot of anger for what we just put her through and sooner or later she was going to let it out. I could tell that she was chanting the whole time we were driving to the safe house. I could see her lips moving. She waited until we got to our safe house to get loud. Boy did she get loud. She really had a set of pipes on her, and she was not holding back. As we were escorting her into the house, she was yelling for help as loud as she could. At one point she decided to break away from our security's grasp and as soon as she figured out that was not going to work, she kicked her mother in the leg. The security guy swooped her up into his arms and in the house they went. It was funny to see the look on her face. She was not expecting anyone to lay a hand on her. Boy was she surprised. I told her what she just did was not going to work so she needed to stay calm. I went on to tell her again if she stayed calm no one would put a hand on her. It was up to her. She came to realize we meant business and she calmed down. I knew then we had our hands full.

The deprogrammers had already arrived and after she was led into her bedroom, they wasted no time in getting started with her. She went on to do what most cult kids do and that was to chant for the first two days. It was not until she figured out that was not working, she stopped. After that she got quiet. I was waiting for her to lash out again. She did not. She finally fell asleep. I knew the hours she had been working she would sleep for hours, and we were going to let her. I decided to take advantage of her sleeping and take the parents grocery shopping. When I walked into the kitchen, I could sense the relief they were both feeling. They were happy to have this part behind them and so was I. I had been on this case for weeks now and I had been through a lot. It was rewarding to have accomplished so much up to this point in time. Now it was up to the deprogrammers to take it to the finish line. At the grocery store we filled two shopping carts. This food would not last long with about twelve people to feed. We would have to do it again in a couple of days. When we got back Bobbie was still sleeping. When we walked in the door it did not take long for our security staff to dig into the grocery's we just bought. Dealing with the parents and taking them shopping was part of my job along with security and most everything else. I loved my job and I loved these kids. All of us did. Bobbie went on to sleep fifteen hours, and when she woke up, she stayed in bed for another two. She had not been able to sleep like this in years. When she got up, she was not talking to anyone. Not even her mom or dad. Whenever someone started talking to her, she would start chanting again. I told her she had her own bathroom and she could use it whenever she wanted. The look on her face was shock. She had been so brainwashed into believing we were going to torture her, mistreat her and starve her. She did not want to do anything we were asking. I was surprised when I asked her if she wanted to take a shower, she said yes. I was about to find out why she was eager to do so. I led her to the bathroom door, and she went in and shut the door. What she tried to do next we were ready for. First, she tried to lock the door, but we had already turned the doorknobs around so that was not going to work. Next, I could hear her stand up on the toilet seat. She was trying to get out the little window we had screwed shut. When that was all done, I took a female deprogrammer with me into the bathroom. We just stood there waiting for her to make her next move. I told her all the windows were screwed shut and she was not going anywhere. I went on to tell her if she were going to play nice, we would leave her alone to take her shower by herself and if not, her mother would be in to watch her. I turned around and the deprogrammer and myself walked out and shut the door. Now she was left alone to make that decision for herself. She had not been able to make these decisions for herself for many years. I knew she was safe and there was nowhere for her to go.

It did not take long before the water in the shower was turned on. I could hear it bouncing off her. We had already unplugged the exhaust fan so we could hear what was going on in there. She stayed in the shower long enough to use up all the hot water. This was another thing she was not allowed to do in years. I knew she enjoyed it. When she came out of the shower, we could tell that the fifteen hours of sleep and that long shower had calmed her down quite a bit. When she walked into her room her mother had a spread laid out with fruits of different kinds, bagels, two different kind of juices, along with a cup of hot chocolate with marshmallows she liked as a kid. She walked in saw all of this and said nothing. The deprogrammers were sitting there waiting for her. To my surprise they stayed quiet. Truly little time had passed before she would give in to the smell. She did not leave anything on her plate and the deprogrammers just sat there in silence. After she was done, I removed her plate and left her a cold bottle of water. I walked out and shut the door part way. My duty shift was about over, and my replacement was already sitting in a chair outside her bedroom door. Room security gets boring after a while. These deprogrammers would sit and talk for hours. Bobbie was trying to not pay attention. Every once in a while, you could see her start to lose her battle and she would start to chant again. She did not want to hear what was being told to her, but she was having a tough time blocking it out. As I have said in the past most of these deprogrammers have been in a cult before. But not all of them. These two had been. They were the best I had ever been around. The love they had for these kids is beautiful. They know what these kids go through every day of their lives as cult members. They will sit and talk forever, never giving up. They are the best. What we all do is dangerous and illegal, but it does not matter to any of us. We are here for the kids. We will continue to be here for them as long as they need us. It would take about another week for Bobbie to turn the corner and start asking a lot of questions. Within a couple more days she came to realize for the last four years she had been following a false prophet.

One of the reasons I do what I do is because of what Bobbie would do next. The deprogrammers had broken through her mind control, and she was going through the transition that all cult members go through after being deprogrammed. To this day it is still the most beautiful thing I have ever witnessed. Just a couple weeks ago Bobbie had kicked her mother in the leg, and she felt no remorse in doing so. That has all changed. Bobbie asked the deprogrammers if she could see her mom and dad. They said sure. I brought the mother in first, and when she saw her, she started to cry. She got up and started hugging her mother and that made her mother cry. Since both of them were crying I decided to bring in the father. You guessed it, now they are all hugging and crying. Bobbie was telling her mother how sorry she was for kicking her and that made both of them cry. It never gets old seeing families brought back together again.

The deprogrammers sat back and enjoyed the beauty of it all. They spent two more days talking with Bobbie and they told me she was ready to go outside for a walk. I suggested she may feel more comfortable with just one security guy, the mother, and the father and both deprogrammers, and they agreed. I was elected to be that one security guy. This was going to be the real test to see how well the deprogrammers had done their jobs. I was sure we would encounter other people; we usually do. If the deprogrammers said she was ready, then that was good enough for me. I trusted them with my life. It was a cool day but nice. We had walked for about an hour without any problems. We did encounter a few people walking their dogs and at one point a police officer drove by. He was going slowly enough to wave. Everyone was talking but me. I needed to listen for any kind of remarks that would tell me we were in trouble. It was nice listening to all the plans that were being made. I was glad to hear both parents were going to drop everything to spend whatever time she would need as a family. Vacation was brought up and plans were in the works from all three of them. We returned to the safe house without any problems. All the rest of the team was glad to see us walk through the door. That evening the parents took me aside and gave me a hug. That happens to me a lot. The next day we transported both parents and Bobbie to our rehab center. A month later they all returned home to pack their bags and leave for vacation. I wish I were going with them. The cult lost another one to the good guys and I could not be happier. There would be one more bright child with a future. On to my next adventure.

CHAPTER FOURTEEN

MOONIE CULT: MARIA

This story takes me from Florida all the way to Seattle Washington. I received a call from Sara from my office. She gave me the address of a couple of mothers that were asking for our help. But there was a catch. They were asking if we would take this job on as a charity case. I did not even ask why. I flew out the next day and met with the two guardians of who I will call Maria. Maria had been adopted by two women that were wife and wife. If I am saying that correctly. They both seemed nice and polite. When I pulled onto their property what I saw did not make any sense. There were four of the most beautiful horses I have ever seen. Parked in the driveway were not one but two jaguars' convertibles and a thirty-six-foot motor home. Sitting beside that was a brand-new horse trailer. If this was a charity case, I must be Santa Claus. We sat on the veranda and were served by what seemed to be the maid. I sat and listened to their story. When they were done talking the question I had to ask was, why am

I being asked to do this as a charity case with all this stuff sitting in the driveway? They told me they would rather not get into it right now. I was floored. They wanted me to trust them when they could not or would not tell me what was going on. I told them I had traveled thousands of miles at my expense, and this was their answer. I got up and started to excuse myself and walk away, when one of the mothers started to cry. I stopped and stood there and waited for something to be said from either one of them. All I got was total silence. I did not tell them I would never turn down anyone that needed my help, but I needed honesty from the start. I started to walk away again, when one of the mothers spoke up.

I was told the reason I was being asked to do this for little or no money was because these two women were used to their lifestyles and they did not want to change anything. I did not know what to say. I was speechless. I excused myself and I told them I needed time to take this all in. I could not believe what I was hearing. I drove off and found a motel room and checked in. I needed to run this by another female and Sara came to mind. I called the office and Sara answered. After explaining to her what I saw and heard, I needed to know if I was thinking crazy or not. Her statement to me was, we were dealing with a couple of buttheads and I agreed. The problem I was dealing with was I had a young woman out there somewhere that needed my help. Was I going to let the greed of her two mothers stand in the way of helping her out? I was starting to not like these two women, and I like everyone. I needed to sleep on it. I called Marias parents and told them I would meet them in the morning and give them my answer. I already knew what I was going to say. I just did not want to start this case feeling the way I felt. Tomorrow things should look a little clearer. After a good night sleep and a great dinner, I headed back over to their farm. I did not know how I was going to be greeted. I knocked on the door and the maid answered. I could see both of them standing there waiting for the door to be opened. They asked me in, and I declined. I did not want to see any more than I had already seen. I was sure there were signs of money everywhere. The reasons we do this kind of work has never been about money and I was not going to start here. I did not give either one of them the chance to say anything. I told them I was here for Maria. I said I would take on this case for her. I would do everything in my power to find her and remove her from whatever cult she had gotten caught up in.

After gathering all the information from her parents, I went about the business of finding her. What her parents knew was Maria had met some nice kids and she quit her job and that was the last they had seen or heard from her. At that point in time there were at least five well known cults groups in this area. Her parents gave me Marias journal that she kept up to the point she disappeared. She wrote about how much love and peace she is feeling being around these new friends. That was the end of what she wrote. But it was enough for me. I was betting on her new friends being Moonies. But where was she? It is a big world out there, and little to go on. I have worked in this area before but not with the Moonie cult. I had a lot of work ahead of me. Some of this work I could have done back at my office, but it was too late now. It took me a few days to locate an address of a house the Moonies used a long time ago. This address was a two-hour drive from here. I was hoping for a house closer to this area. But for now, this is what I have to work with. After driving for over two hours I finally arrived at the address I had. When I pulled onto the street the house, I was looking for had been torn down. I waited around for the mail man hoping to get a lead. The only information I could get was there had been a fire and the people who lived in that house were away during the fire. That was it. I would spend the next four days trying to come up with a Moonie house anywhere. All my leads were dead ends. I checked with the police and the local college. I did come across two other cults working in this area but no Moonies. I checked with the local parent group and they could not give me any more information than they already had. I walked the malls, the shopping centers and I even checked in on an old folks' home and nothing. I staked out the post office for a couple of days. Everything I was trying was not leading me anywhere.

Maria had been gone for a few months before her mothers had contacted the parent group for help. She could be anywhere. I made an appointment with a lawyer in the local area, and two hundred dollars later I found out she had not been arrested or had not gotten any traffic tickets. Her mother said she did not have any credit cards they knew about. I spent the next two weeks driving around trying to get lucky. I contacted my office and they did come up with a couple of possible leads. I decided to look around a couple of smaller towns that were only fifty miles away. There was an incident that happened a while back where an elderly man chased a couple of cult kids away from his laundromat and in doing so, he keeled over from a heart attack. It hit all the newspapers. Not having a place to start from makes things a lot harder, and I was relying on a small bit of luck. I drove the distance to that town and located the post office and the laundromat. I did not believe they would still be around this area, but I needed to do something positive and this was it. I spent the next two days looking around and asking a lot of questions to anyone that would listen. Somehow, and do not ask me why, I ended up at the library. I inquired into any information that could help me find where the cult might have moved to after the heart attack incident. I was told there was a lady that worked here, and she knew all about what went on. But she was not due back to work until tomorrow. I had to travel thirty more miles to a town with a motel. After checking in and putting together what I did know, I came to the conclusion if I didn't come up with anything soon I would have to stop looking for her, or wait until I could get a better handle on where the Moonie locations might be. Spinning my wheels was not my cup of tea and one thing I had learned a long time ago running in circles does not usually get you very far. Well hopefully the next day would bring some light to this crazy hunt. I showed up at the library at ten a.m. and met with the nicest lady. She talked and I listened. She told me her grandson had done a paper on the cult that was living in this small town a while back. She said part of his paper was to find out the truth about their teachings and he followed them around watching them solicit. He told his grandmother they often stopped at a house in another town ten miles away. Yes, she knew the address. She had no problem in giving me the address, and she went on to say right after the incident with the heart attack the cult left in the middle of the night and no one has seen them since. I asked her if her grandson had ever returned to the other address he had, and she told him to stay away from there. She said he usually did what she said. I thanked her and then I drove the ten miles to the address she gave me. When I arrived, there was no vans in the driveway and the town was to small to have a motel. I decided to spend the night in my car. I waited until around ten a.m. and no one showed up. I was not going anywhere until I had proof of who lived in that house. At daybreak I went up their driveway and removed their trash from their trash can and put it in the back of my car. I decided to wait for another few hours just in case anyone would show up. No one did. It was time for me to find a larger town with a motel, and after checking in I went through their trash and I found the proof I was looking for. It did not give me the correct information I was looking for but there was enough information for me to know it was definitely a house used by the Moonie cult. What I was looking at was a list of names that were given to each cult member living in this house. The problem was these were cult given names. The cult gave each member new names when they joined. These were not the real names. I always knew this cult did this, but it is the first time I have seen them written down. It was hard to tell if any of these names were female. This was the break I was looking for. Along with a little luck I might be in business. There was a total of ten names on the list I had and that was the magic number the Moonie cult used when they would do what was called mobile fund raising. I was hoping I was wrong because if that were what this group was doing, they could be gone for weeks or even longer. My plan was clear from here. At least for a few more days. I would stop by this house at the end of the day and stake out the post office during the day. Hopefully, something would come of either one of my ideas. If this group were soliciting locally, they would be out during the day and they would be returning home at night. The only thing was, am I at the right Moonie house? Only time would tell. As I have stated in some of my earlier stories one of the jobs of the Moonie drivers is to drop off all his cult people to different locations in the morning. When they had time, they would pick up their mail from a post office box. At the end of the day he would drive around and pick everyone back up. This adds up to a ten to fourteen-hour day for all of them. Everyday. I believe there is another Moonie house close by. I need to find out as much as I can over the next few days. I decided to stick with my plan for the next five days. By the end of the fifth day I still had very little to go on. They could be hundreds or thousands of miles away. By the time, the excitement of finding the Moonie house wore off, I was still working off my dime and that was money I did not think I would ever see back. The only thing keeping me going was the thought of Maria. I was dedicated to finding her and it did not matter how long it took or how much money I spent. I was about to find out how much patience I really had. I called my office to see if any information had come in that would speed things up. I had been looking for Maria for over a month now and things were not looking particularly good. I knew anytime now I would be encountering the police. I had been in a neighborhood watch area and it was only a matter of time before they would show up. Parked up the street from a Moonie house night after night was sure to bring them around. I was about to find out how right I was.

It was the next evening and I was parked up the street from the Moonie house. One police car pulled in front of me and one to the rear. I had my window down and my badge ready for them. I do believe they knew why I was here. They were just doing their job. It was not helpful they had their lights flashing and the road blocked. So much for trying to keep a low profile. I had been through this several times before, so it did not take them long to be satisfied with my answers. One of the officers drove off and the other one decided to stick around. The second officer moved his car next to the curb and turned his lights off. Then he walked up to my car and stuck his head in the window. What blew my mind was what he did next. He stood around and talked for over an hour. He wanted to know what it was like to be a private eye/bodyguard. He knew just about everything about the kind of work I did, and he was fascinated to hear it from the horse's mouth as they say. I might as well come out and spill the beans because he was not going anywhere soon. I knew how to handle this kind of situation, but this was a lot more intense hearing some of the things coming out of my mouth. Even I started feeling like a real superhero of some kind. I knew I had given him enough information for him to leave. But he had to do what all the police officers do and that was to tell me if I had any intentions of breaking the law he would return and arrest me, as he turned and walked away laughing. I did find it amusing. But I was glad it was over. I waited until he pulled away to start my car. Just as I was ready to leave the Moonie van drove past me and into their driveway. What a bit of luck. If that officer had not stayed around as long as he did, I would have been miles away from here. This is how it happens sometimes; you just never know. This was that little bit of luck I was hoping for.

I drove down the street a little closer to the house. The streetlight gave off enough light so I could see ten kids get out of the van, and yes, there were boys and girls. I still believed there was another Moonie house close by. I think this group was using the other house to stay in while the other group was out mobile fund raising. It was only a guess. This group must have been soliciting locally and they were using the other house and post office box. It started to make sense to me. It would explain why I had not seen hide nor hair of them up to now. It was important to me because if I was right this group should be leaving for their mobile fund raising soon. If they had been soliciting all day, then their driver would have to get some sleep before they could leave again. I was hoping I had figured it out. It was time to head back to my room and get some sleep. I slept well and I was back at their house early the next morning. When I arrived, they were loading their van. With everything they had packed, we were going on a road trip. They parked their van too close to their house for me to see who got into the van. Here we go, they are pulling out of the driveway. I was glad I slept well last night because we were going to be on the road for some time. Who knows when I would get a chance to sleep again? We had been driving all day and I was tired. We drove far enough to be out of the state of Washington. A few miles down the road we turned onto a gravel road. This road was in bad shape. Top speed was fifteen miles an hour, we were in the country now. There were so many potholes it was hard staying on the road. Along with that it was a dusty road and it was making it hard not to be noticed. I was hoping they did not decide to turn around, there was nowhere for me to go. I was getting low on gas and it did not look like there was anything around for miles. We were not traveling extremely far at this speed. Thank goodness for rental cars. It was not very long before the dirt road turned to pavement. Within ten minutes we were pulling into a service station.

As the driver of the van was getting gas a few of the cult kids had gone into the store. None of them was Maria. I waited up the road while they got gas. Just as soon as their van started pulling out of the service station, I pulled in and got gas. I could not take the time to fill it up completely because they were already out of sight. After a few gallons I was back on the road hoping to catch up. The farther I drove the more the roads turned off to the right and to the left. They could have turned onto any one of them. Around the next bend sitting in a driveway was the van. It was empty. I drove past their van until I could find a place to park close to their house. Now I was asking myself why did they get gas at night? Are they going anywhere tonight? When was the gas station going to close and when would it reopen? These are the questions I had no answers for. I decided to go back to the gas station and finish filling my tank. I was hungry and I did not care if it was coming out of a can. When I got back to the station, I found out they were closing in ten minutes and they would be reopening at seven.

That answered those questions. Now I had gotten gas and some food, I was on my way back to their house. Directly across the street from their house was an old baseball field. It had a few outbuildings that were not being used. It made great cover and I had a great view of their house. Timing is everything. If I had not had to get gas when they did, I could have seen everyone get out of the van. Now all I could do is watch and wait.

One of the things my readers need to know when it comes to religious cults, sometimes we must throw logic out the window and go with our old gut feelings. With that being said, my plan is to stay awake all night. I do not want to take any chances of missing anything. I am hoping to not see the police tonight. Whatever was going to happen I must be ready for it. It is a beautiful and peaceful night. Being in the country makes things so surreal. The sound of the crickets, and the moon was so bright. It made keeping an eye on the Moonie house a little easier. I was hoping to see Maria walk out the door. The lights in the house went out, and it looked like it was going to stay that way. I decided to take a short nap with my windows down. I was not that close to their house but with the night so still I thought I would wake up from the smallest noise. It did not take me long to fall asleep and I slept soundly. This sleep became valuable to me as time went on.

It was morning and I did not want to be seen sitting here in the daylight, so I drove around the corner and parked. I got out of my car and walked over to the baseball field to see who was getting into the van. It was seven a.m. and the front door opened, and everyone was walking onto the porch. So far, no Maria. I had a decision to make and I needed to do it soon. If the van leaves without Maria in it, do I follow the van? Or do I stick with these two Moonie houses? So far things have been crazy. Hopefully when the time comes, I will make the right decision. That decision needed to be made in the next ten minutes because the van is loaded, and they are ready to drive away. As they loaded the van, I counted ten people. It was ten people that got out of the van the night before. Maria was not one of them. I ran back to my car and got ready to follow them, wherever that may lead me. I was not going to start second guessing myself. I was going to stick to what I had been doing and hope I got lucky. We were heading back past the gas station and I was glad they did not take that bumpy road. Six hours had passed, and we had not stopped yet. The farther I followed them the better chance they would find out someone was following them. Again, I was hoping for a stop soon, but it did not happen. They just kept on driving. We were a long way from where we had started, and I could not think of any reason for them to turn around but turn around they did. They used the median strip to turn around and now they were heading straight for me. There was not any place or time to get out of the way. I did the only thing I could think of, that was to jump out of my car and raise the hood up and I ran to the other side of the car. I was hoping they would not get a good look at the front of my car with the hood up. To them I should look like a stranded motorist on the side of the road. The windows in the van were tinted so the only person that could get a good look at me would be the driver. When they drove by me, they were chanting and were not paying any attention to me. I closed my hood, jumped into my car, and drove through the grass and the median strip. I was back on track and no one was the wiser. It was not long before they drove a little farther and then turned around again. They were headed straight towards me once again. I thought they were going to do that, so I was ready for them. I already had a spot to turn into and by the time they reached me I would be out of their sight. It was not long before they drove right past me. They were still chanting when they went by. Once again, I followed them. I could not afford for them to do this again, but I knew that they would not. I knew what was coming next. It did not take long before they were off the highway and pulling into a mall parking lot. They dropped off two kids and a few minutes later we were driving out of the lot and down a side street. Soon he was pulling into a post office. After retrieving their mail, we were back on the road. This was a good thing. Somewhere close by is a Moonie house and he is going to lead me right to it. I love it when I am right. Within five minutes he was pulling into another Moonie house. I was certain since he led me here, he did not know he was being followed. I was glad. The best is yet to come. When he pulled into the driveway out walked Maria. I could not believe my eyes, I finally got lucky. I pulled into a body shop across from this house. I felt I could stay parked here for some time without being noticed. Things were looking up. Maria helped the driver unload the van into the garage and then they both went into the house. I did not believe they would be going anywhere soon, so I headed to the closest motel. I knew what to expect next. After a good shower and more food than I could eat I took a nap. Maria and the driver were not going anywhere until it was time to pick up the kids at the shopping center. I had been following these kids for some time now and I was pleased my hunch paid off. Sticking to my gut feelings was the right thing to do. Being in this type situation before helped. My work had just begun.

I contacted my office and told Sara the good news and asked her to get my team ready. She told me they were all standing in front of her and were ready to go to work. I told her I would call her back the next day but just in case to book the flights for everyone for two days from now. She said she was glad to. All I had to do now was contact Marias two mothers and give them the news. I decided to wait until I woke up from my nap. I slept for a few hours before I was up putting together what I was going to do next. I will share my plan with you all in a minute. I placed the call to Marias two mothers and let them know what I found out and they were thrilled to hear the news. I informed them to hop into one of their two jaguars and head in my direction. Well, onto what I figured would happen next.

Since Maria and the driver put everything away in the garage, I believed they had plans to stick close to home and work the malls and the shopping centers, or even the colleges, soliciting Reverend Moon's goods. It was time for the college students to return to school and there would be new students arriving any day now. Since Maria had not been on the streets soliciting, I was banking on her to be working with the recruiting staff which Moon had thousands of. It made sense. Now all I needed to do was confirm my beliefs. The next day should tell the story. If I was right, by tonight there should be two vans parked in their driveway. For now, all I could do was wait. After grabbing a few things, I headed back to the house. It was starting to get dark and they should be arriving soon. Just like clockwork they pulled into the driveway. It takes a while but after working around this cult it becomes easier to predict what their moves will be. Well the first van had pulled into the driveway and soon the other one should follow. I was right. The other van just drove by me and is pulling into the driveway now. The first van had ten kids in it, the second had only one plus the driver. Just what I was hoping for. All my hard work and many days on the road up to this point seems to be paying off. These next steps are up to Maria and her sidekicks to tell me what will happen next. I decided to hang around for a few more hours until I was satisfied, they were not going to be soliciting tonight. It was a good thing I decided to stick around because right after dinner out walked Maria and two other kids. They got into their van and drove off. I followed. What happened next was easy to figure out, they were headed for the college town, and into the bar district. I had seen all I needed to see.

Back to my motel room. When I walked in the phone was ringing and it was Sara. She told me that every one of my teammates should be arriving tonight. I was not expecting them for one more day, but that is Sara. She is always thinking ahead and pulling off some of the smartest moves. She has always tried to keep the chaos out of my life. In this business that is big. I had a couple of options for removing Maria from the group. One in the daytime and one at night. I would make that decision after meeting with my team tonight. It was four o'clock when my team arrived. Shortly after that Marias parents called my office and told Sara they would be arriving at my location in one hour. I was starting to feel some relief from the monkey on my back. It is really rewarding every time I get that first look at who I am looking for. It never gets old. In this case everything was against me from the start. Not having a place to start and add to it the length of time I spent searching without any luck, it does get discouraging, and that makes the monkey even heavier. Most parents expect a lot from us, and it is understandable, these are their children we are after. It is tough on them not knowing what the end result is going to be. Well for now that is in the past. I need to focus on making the right moves. Nothing but the thought of Maria can get in my head. My team is here, and Marias parents have arrived. I am starting to see an end in sight. Life is looking rather good. During my time searching for Maria, Sara has been working on getting a safe house ready. It is a hard thing to do not knowing where were going to end up. She always comes through for us and I know she will this time. Like I have said in the past it really is not that hard to figure out what moves the cult will make next. The hard part is separating Maria from her teammates safely. My teammates are the best and they will get the job done. What I am counting on is for Maria to get dropped off with just one person. And then her driver would leave and return for them a few hours later. This would leave us with just one person to have to deal with. They were left there without any transportation so their chances of getting any help soon would be slim. All we need is a few seconds. I was working on a plan for this to happen. Once again, I need to run my plan past my teammates and see what they think. It must be unanimous for us to move forward.

A short time had passed, and I had everyone together, and I went over my plan to pick Maria up. We would use our same method as we had used in the past but this time, I was going to us one of Marias mothers to distract Maria. I needed someone to draw Maria off guard for a few seconds. I believed having her mother show her face would give us the time we needed. My experience working around this cult gives me the advantage. I was going to use that advantage to my favor. I was counting on Marias driver to drop both of his kids off in one spot. And within a few seconds he should be driving away. Hopefully. I would have followed her around for a couple more days to get her routine down before bringing in the rest of my team. But I have been following them for so long I could not afford to take the chance of having my cover blown. If that happened, it would be all over. I just could not take that chance and my teammates agreed. The worst-case scenario had been worked out by my teammates and I put all my confidence in them. I appreciated the fresh insights my team had brought to the table. It had been a long case and to tell you the truth I was starting to get a little frazzled. But this is what we do, and we always do it together. I knew when the time was right my adrenaline would kick in and I would be myself again. Normally we would have already known where we were going to pick her up. That would only require me to sit and wait at her house for her to leave for work and everyone else would be at the pickup site. Not this time. It was going to take all ten of us to follow her from her house and be ready in a split second. If ever there was a team to pull this off its these guys. With that being said, a lot could go wrong. The amount of people we had with us we would need too many cars to follow her around for too long. Trying to get through traffic especially not knowing where and when she was going to be dropped off was a crap shoot. Therefore, knowing ahead of time makes more sense.

Well here we go. We have three cars ready for our pursuit. One of the mothers was with me in the front seat. I had to choose which one of the mothers I would use in this part of the operation. That choice came easy for me. I chose the only mother that showed any emotion when we first met. I picked the one that did the crying. Even though I was not fond of either one of them I had to make a choice, and I did. We were about to find out how all of this was going to go down because their van was pulling out of the driveway with Maria and two of her teammates. They did not go far before they drove into the far side of a well-known coffee shop. This is what I was hoping would happen. By this time, they had gotten out of the van and stood there chanting. Now all we needed to do was wait for the van driver to drive away. He did not. All three of my staff members had already started walking towards Maria. The van was still sitting there, and I was starting to get concerned. Timing is everything. I cannot make my move if the van is still there. We, as a group, had discussed this happening and were prepared to back off if need be. We could always make another attempt if we had to. We were all on the same page and even though we were coming from a couple different directions we would work as a team. Just as I was about to call my staff and abort the pickup the van drove off. He was no longer a threat. That was my cue to make my move. Without hesitation I pulled up next to Maria and her sidekick. I was hoping that Maria was not so caught up in her chanting that it would block out her mother's voice. It did not. She turned around to respond to her mother's voice and she was stunned. That was the distraction we needed to make it happen. It gave the one security guard enough time to detain her teammate, while the other two security guys escorted Maria into the back seat of my car. By this time, our back up car drove up and assisted the security guy that had Marias teammate. He was also there to stop anyone who might try to interfere in case Maria would decide to cry out for help. We only had about seven seconds if we were going to pull this off and get away undetected. To my calculations it took about five seconds for this to happen and we were pulling out of the parking lot. I hope I have been able to put you in our shoes for this adventure. If so, I have done my job. These thoughts run through our heads, are we going to get caught, is something going to go wrong, will Maria get away? These are only some of the things that go through our minds and it happens every time. The adrenaline rushing through our bodies keeps us focused and keeps us doing everything perfectly, so no one gets hurt.

Sara had our safe house all set up, but it was a two-hour drive to reach our location. We were gone from the pickup sight and it did not seem like anyone was the wiser. My back up car caught up with me and that was a good sign. Maria was doing what we expected her to do and that was to chant. That is ok with me. The longer she chanted the closer we got to the safe house. At least she was not making a scene. I was not in the mood for her to start misbehaving, but I was ready for it, we all were. She did not even yell at her mother. All she did for the two-hour drive was chant. We arrived at our safe location. We were able to pull straight into the garage where the deprogrammers were waiting. Security escorted Maria into the house and she went in quietly. I asked her before we took her to her bedroom if she had to use the bathroom and she said nothing. She continued to chant all night and into the next day until she fell asleep. Over the next few days, she would show off her anger at will. She was letting us know she was not happy. What she would learn in the next few days is that she had not been happy in quite some time. The deprogrammers did their job and let her express her anger. This was the first time in a long time she was able to express any of her true feelings, and she had a few. As security we are responsible for everyone's safety. We would be keeping an eye on Maria twenty-four hours a day. The Moonies are not as violent as some of the other cults but when a person is under mind control anything is possible. She would chill out over the next few days. She slept, ate, and showered when she wanted to. She did what all cult kids do and that was to hang onto her beliefs in her so-called Messiah for as long as she could. She thought she knew everything there was to know about Moon. She was in for a surprise. As I have written in other stories these deprogrammers have walked the walk. And in many cases, they have done it for years. Maria was in good hands and was being treated very well. She was still stubborn until the deprogrammers got her to see the real side of her so-called Messiah. It would take another two weeks before she would denounce the cult that she had been caught up in. She went off to our rehabilitation center with both of her mother's where she would stay for thirty days. I am pleased to say that

Moon lost another young adult to the good guys, and that makes me happy. The whole adventure has taken many twists but the twist that is most important is that Maria is at home and is doing well and for that it was all worth it. And for the two mothers that insisted on a break in the cost, I gave it to them...five dollars off. On to the next case.

CHAPTER FIFTEEN

MOONIE CULT: SANDY

I had been working at one of our rehab centers and having a good time as usual. I received a package in the mail from a parent group. The note inside said there was a young girl that was in trouble, and her parents were asking for our help. As I looked over her photos all I could think about was my own children. I soon put myself at ease knowing they were safe. I am one of the luckier fathers in the world. I do not have to worry about them getting caught in any religious cult. But what if they did? I will always keep that thought in the back of my mind. I do it as a reminder to myself at any time or any place they could be taken from me. To tell you the truth, I do not believe I would handle it any better than any of the family's that I have met.

Even though my career is winding down, and soon it will come to an end, I will never give up on any family member that needs my help or cries out for answers. I have always wished I could do more to ease the pain any parents go through when their son or daughter comes up missing.

Sandys' parents live in New York. And after talking to them on the phone, I grabbed a cab and headed for the airport. When I spoke with her parents, I could feel the sadness they felt not knowing what happened to their daughter. The information I received from her parents who I will call the Fergie's was that Sandy always wanted to get into acting and her father had a friend that was a college professor in Berkley California. He had set up an interview with his friend for Sandy. Sandy had an uncle that lived outside San Francisco and he spent a lot of his time out of the country. Sandy had flown out a few weeks ago and was going to stay at her uncles' home while he was away. She would have the use of his car whenever she would need it. The last conversation her mom had with her daughter was two weeks after she arrived in San Francisco. She told her mother she had met some new friends. She said she was having dinner with them. By the time the Fergie's had gotten in touch with us a lot of time had gone by. After my conversation with the Fergie's I did not waste any time. I caught a flight out to San Francisco that same day. After arriving I grabbed a rental car then checked into a motel. I had worked in Berkley before, and I am familiar with what goes on there. Sandy is an incredibly beautiful twenty-two-year-old girl, and Berkley is full of twenty-two-year-old girls. The first place I wanted to check out was her uncles' home. When I arrived at his home and got out of my car what grabbed my attention was at the base of the side door there was a broken clay flowerpot. The dirt from the pot was piled up high enough if anyone went in or out of the door it would have moved that pile. There was no sign of that. I could see through the windows at the side door, and all the furniture had sheets still draped over them. It was obvious that no one had been staying on this side of the house in a while. Most of the houses in this area are built on the side of a hill. As I walked around the house there was no way to enter the home except the side door. By the looks of the front door it had not been used in years. I was unable to see into the house from this side. The last place I looked was in the garage. The side door of the garage was unlocked. When I opened the door there were not any cars inside. It did not look like anyone had been in or out in some time. What I concluded was the flowerpot had been knocked over possibly by a stray animal. There was not any sign that Sandy had been here. I called the Fergie's back in New York to find out what kind and color of car his brother owned. They were not sure, but they believed it was a convertible, possibly tan and black in color. That is what I am going to keep an eye open for. I wanted to check out Berkley before it got any later. When I arrived, it was just like I remembered it. Young people everywhere. Picking out Sandy was not going to be easy. Within the first thirty minutes I saw at least one hundred Sandys walking around. Being a young man myself, and being surrounded by hundreds of young females, it was not hard for me to enjoy myself. But and there is always a but, I had to focus, and after I got my hormones in check, I continued to do my job without any luck. If she had gotten caught up in the Moonies as I had suspected, she would be doing one or two things for the cult. It was my guess with the beauty Sandy possessed she was put on the recruiting staff. This college atmosphere was a perfect place for her to do very well. Everything was telling me to stick around.

Being young myself it should not be hard for me to blend in. As the day went on, the more I could see a lack of any cults working this area. I found that to be very odd. There must be something else going on that I was missing. But what? I decided to hang around a little while longer and check out the bars and night clubs and see if any cult kids show up. After having dinner, I walked over to the bar district. I went in and out of all the bars and clubs in walking distance for any signs of the Moonies. I did encounter the Hare Krishna cult, but no Moonies. There is always the chance that they could have been here a few days ago and the police could have run them off. It made sense. It is time to call it a night, so I went back to my motel room. My plan was to get up early and check out Fisherman's Wharf. I also want to go by the uncle's home again.

The next day came early and I was on the move. I did not think that my next location would produce any results. It was just a gut feeling. I went anyway. After walking around there and a few other areas that I was familiar with, I started asking myself is she still in California? It was time for me to head to the uncle's home. It was mid-day, and I did not believe she was going to be there, but it was a shot. Just as I thought no one has been in or out of his driveway. My next move is to head back to Fisherman's Wharf. Hopefully, there would be some action going on there. The Moonies are always there at their slip recruiting new members. Hopefully, Sandy would be among them. I did not believe what I was about to do was a good idea especially after the incident on another case when I had to infiltrate into the Moonie house. I am sure they have pictures of me. They know who I am, after we spoiled the chance for them to take in two million dollars that day. That is a day they will never forget. I must keep my cool and make sure I read every situation perfectly. I parked as close as I could. Walking around here brings back some good and some bad memories. I found an area that would work well, since I was probably going to be sitting here for some time. I did not need any of Moons recruiters approaching me.

I sat down and had a good look of where the Moonie bus would be showing up to take all the new recruit's to dinner. It was close to dinner time so their bus should be arriving anytime now. What happened next, I had to study for a while. What I was expecting was a bus but what pulled up was a van. Standing on the sidewalk across the street from where the van pulled up stood more than thirty new recruits along with five cult leaders. They were waiting for the bus. There were too many new recruits to try to get them all in one van. What was going on? Where is their bus? Before I could put anymore thought into that, their bus pulled up. It did not take very long to get every one of the new recruits into the bus and then they drove off. So, what was the reason for the van? That question got answered right away. Every one of the cult recruiters had gotten on the bus except for one. He was crossing the street and approaching the van. When he got next to the side of the van, the door swung open and what I saw next blew my mind.

Yes, Sandy was sitting there with two of her cult leaders. I also noticed travel bags enough for all of them. That I did not want to see. You are probably asking why would that disturb me? Yes, I did locate Sandy and in a short amount of time. The travel bags meant we were going for a ride and it was not going to be a short one. I really did not think that today was going to be the day I would locate Sandy. It was just a feeling. The bad part was I did not check out of my motel room. Everything I had with me was back in my room. Well there is not any chance of going back there now. They are pulling out of their parking spot. You would think that I would have been smarter than that, but this is one of those times we realize we are human. Boy did I feel stupid. A lot of the streets around this area are one-way streets. For them to be going away from the Moonie house and getting on any highway they had to drive past my parked car. You know, the car I was running back to. I arrived back to my car just in time to get behind them. We were heading for the highway. After getting onto the highway I was three car lengths behind them. If we were going to be traveling as far as I believed we would, I did not want to take the chance of being seen. I honestly believed I would have been back at the end of the day sitting in my motel room wondering what steps I would take the next day to find Sandy. I got lucky I found Sandy and for that I am happy. But I should have been more prepared for anything and I was not. I am hard on myself because it has always kept me on my toes. Not this time. Like I said I got lucky and for that life is good. Nothing wrong with a little luck. I am sure I will be needing more luck as time goes on. Well, it was five o'clock and we are sitting in stop and go traffic. This is not a good time to be on any road going anywhere. Even though I am a few car lengths behind them if they decide to get out of traffic, I could not take the chance of following them. They have been known to drive across the median strip and if they decide to do so following them would be almost impossible. We were not going anywhere nor is anyone else. The question is where are we going and why? Time had passed and we did not travel extremely far. I really did not know what to expect next. I was hoping for another Moonie house close by. Only time would tell. It has been four hours since we got onto this highway and now, we were getting off the exit. A few minutes later we were driving through a small town and turning onto a side street. The road we turned onto was a dead-end road. I pulled off onto the side of the road. They drove three houses farther before pulling into a driveway. What was I going to do next? Do I leave and find a motel to get some sleep? When are they going to leave? Is this home for them for while? A lot of unanswered questions were running through my head. What would you do knowing what you know? What I am going to do is go on past experiences and stick to my gut feelings. I am going to sit here and wait to see if any other vans show up. There is always the chance they could drive off in the middle of the night, but I did not think so. Unless there is someone in the house that has slept eight hours, they were not going to drive off anywhere.

There were not any lights on in the house when they pulled in, and no vehicles in the driveway. For what I could see they had no garage. I believe they are in for the night. I really need to get some sleep and I need a change of clothes. And of course, some dinner. I decided to hang around for a little while and see if anything change. It did not take me long to figure out that getting a motel around here was not going to happen. No matter which direction I went this area was not big enough to warrant a motel. It was too late to do anything about getting some clean clothes, but I was able to find some food and supplies. I did have a little more energy after eating something, but I was too tired to go any farther. I called my office and left a message for Sara to call the motel in San Francisco where I left all my belongings. I needed them to pack up my stuff and store it for me until I had a chance to return for it.

I decided to head back to the Moonie house and find some place to keep an eye on the house and try to get some sleep. When I arrived, nothing had changed. Their van was still in the driveway and all the lights in the house were out. Seeing this I felt good about getting some sleep. No one was going to leave at least until morning. When I was here the first time, I did not notice there was an alley that ran behind their house. It made for a perfect spot to sit and watch, or sleep. My plan was to stay awake if I could, but I knew better. I do not even remember turning my engine off. I slept like a baby and I was up in time to see Sandy and her teammates load into their van and drive off. It was seven o'clock sharp. As I drove down the alley in pursuit of them, I saw a tan convertible parked beside a utility shed. This had to be her uncle's car. I would later call Mr. Fergie and let him know where his brother's car was sitting. The cult had not taken the time to move the car, but it would not be much longer until they moved it onto their farm. It took me a few blocks to catch up with their van and within a few minutes we were turning onto the same highway we were on yesterday. We were driving away from San Francisco. It was not until six hours had passed before they turned into a filling station. While they pumped gas some of the kids went inside and grabbed lunch to go. Sandy never left the van. Their van pulled away from the gas pumps and parked. It was lunch time for them. This gave me enough time to get some of the things that I was going to need that I did not have. As I stood in line getting some chicken from the deli their van drove off. I had no time to stand in line. I sat everything down and ran back to my car. I could see them ahead of me getting onto the highway and heading in the same direction as before.

We were heading across the state of California and I did not believe we were going to stop anytime soon. I had that gut feeling that before this was all over, we would be out of California. Unless they decide to stop and establish a routine, removing Sandy from this cult was going to be impossible. I wish I knew where that stop was going to take place, I could have my crew waiting at that end, and we could put an end to this chase. But until then it was going to be the same, keep pursuing them wherever that takes me. We had been driving for hours and I was praying this was going to end soon. I did not know how much longer I could get away with following them without being caught. Sooner or later even the best Private investigator runs out of luck. Besides, I was overdue for a shower and a change of clothes. Just before dark we were turning off the highway and were driving through some small towns. It was becoming extremely hard to follow them. On a few different occasions I would have to stop at a traffic light, and being behind another car, all I could do was watch them drive away. On more than one occasion I had to pull into different businesses and find a way around the traffic that was in front of me. I did not dare run any red lights in these small towns. If I were to get caught, I would lose them for good. I just could not take that chance. After almost losing them a couple times I caught up with them again just as they were turning at a four way stop sign. Boy did I get lucky to see their direction change. A couple more miles down the road was a smaller town. They drove down a one-way street and pulled into a driveway. I was happy to see this. I was able to see down to the end of their road. I parked my car and walked down the sidewalk to get a better look. It really felt good to get out of the car and stretch. I watched as everyone got out of the van and with the porch light on, I could see everyone go into the house, including Sandy. I was relieved. What I noticed right away when we arrived at this small town, there was a fairly good size fair going on. Some of the side streets had already been blocked off for what looked like a parade that may be coming through soon. I wasted no time in driving to a motel I had passed two streets away. Finally, I was going to be able to stop and put my thoughts together. It was my belief that they would be soliciting Moons goods tonight at the fair. Up to this point they had not taken any time to stop and pull in any money for their cult and this was very unusual. Their cult leaders that were traveling with them would have to answer to higher up what their cash intake was and so far, it has been 0 dollars. I was lucky to get the last room available in this town and it was in walking distance from all the action. Every person that lived in this town had already started lining up the sides of the road with their lawn chairs. Blending in was no problem.

After a hot shower and a quick dinner, I was able to walk next door and buy the well needed clothes I had to have. I knew that they would not be leaving soon. The road they were staying on just got blocked off. I felt comfortable enough to get a short nap in. Whether or not Sandy would be soliciting Moons goods tonight at the fair was going to be up to her cult leader. Only time would tell. Regardless if they did or did not, they would be either resting or taking in the fair tonight. Not much of a chance of anyone going anywhere tonight. I was able to sleep well until my alarm went off. I had set it for two hours. Now it was time to see what was going to happen. I walked down the street towards the cult house, and a lot of people were sitting on the porch, including Sandy. At the rear of the house were two more Moonie vans parked up against the house. A few minutes later they were all walking towards me. I was forced to walk around the back of one of the houses on my side of the road, hoping that no one was at home. It took a while for them all to pass by me and reach the end of the block. What I saw next did not make any sense. Not only did they not have anything in their hands to pawn off on all these town folks, but they were embracing these town folks with hugs. There was no doubt that they knew these people. What the heck was going on? This is just not normal that these cult leaders would allow their kids to act like they are acting. Not taking the chance to take in thousands of dollars in a short amount of time was unheard of. And to spend their time just enjoying themselves was crazy. This was just not done. I would soon find out why.

Before I left the motel room, I contacted Sara at my office to let her know that I had located Sandy and to let her parents know as well. I told them not to get excited. We were nowhere close to removing her from her cult. At least not with this many people hanging around. The Fergie's had to be patient and so did I. When I saw Sandy standing on the front porch, I just wanted to walk down the road, throw her over my shoulder and walk away. But it was only a dream. Boy that would make a wonderful end to this story. But back to reality.

After the parade went by everyone walked across the street and into the fair grounds. I followed. After getting into the fair grounds it all made sense to me. This was no ordinary fair. What I was seeing was a couple thousand young men with shave heads with a ponytail sticking out the back of their heads and a couple thousand young females just hanging around. This was not a fair this was a Moonie retreat. I was smack dab in the middle of thousands of cult members and at least a couple hundred of Moons security staff. I was in hell.

It was time for me to get the hell out of here. I have burned too many bridges with this cult, and I had no right to put myself in this situation. It was not only crazy but extremely dangerous. No one knew where I was and if I were to get approached by this cult, things could be over for me. I wasted no time getting back to my motel, my safe grounds. After speaking to the woman at the front desk I was told this goes on every year. She said this was the first year for the parade. To my knowledge none of the parent groups knew about this place because if they did, we would have been told to stay clear of the area. It is just my luck that I find out the hard way. Whatever was going to take place here I wanted no part of. I saw enough of Moons security staff to tell me that he himself would be attending this hoopla. I could not believe I had walked right into this on my own. All the signs were there right in front of me, but I did not see them. After getting over the initial shock of being right in the middle of all of this, I do have to say I was glad it happened. It put everything into place. No more questions for me. All of them had been answered. I am not ashamed to say I did not know what was going to happen next. I needed to find out what the cult plans were for Sandy without the thousands of cult kids and Moons security staff finding out about me again. If I ever needed a miracle or any luck this would be a good time for it.

This is one of those times that I wished I had someone to watch my back. So far, I have gotten myself out of some crazy situations without too much harm, but nothing this intense. I decided to not think about it anymore tonight. Tomorrow should bring some more light to this crazy situation. I was doing this all for Sandy and her parents and I needed to stay focused on that. Following her from here on out will be dangerous and it will have its ups and downs. I do not want to be the person that has to make the call to the Fergie's and let them know that I blew everything and the chances of them ever seeing their daughter again would be very slim. If that were to happen the cult would put her so far into hiding, she would never be seen again. It has happened in the past and I do not want to ever go through that again. There are no guarantees in this business, but we are professional, and failure is not an option. After a good night sleep, I was up early and had checked out of my motel room. From what I was able to see this fair had concluded. They had started to take down all the temporary buildings and everything suggested it would be back to normal soon. I walked down to the corner where the Moonie house was and things there were starting to happen. The cult kids were packing the vans. Shortly they would leaving. This little town was not going to bring them in any money, so they would be heading elsewhere. These cult leaders would not allow the kids to stay idle any longer. They would have to find a location big enough to support their free money. Or should I say Moons money. Soon they will be leaving, but in what direction? I had a fairly good idea which direction they would be heading. I knew the last time they had gotten gas; they should be filling up soon if their plans are to drive far. I decided to take the chance and sit across the street from the gas station and wait. I was banking on Sandy being in the same van with the same kids she started with. It had been one hour since I parked across the street. I was starting to wonder if I had made the right choice or did, they leave in the other direction. I knew better than to start doubting myself. It usually did not get me far. I was going off what I thought was right and soon I would find out. Or back to the drawing board. Finally, both vans pulled in and got gas. Only a couple of kids got out of the vans and went inside. Sandy was not one of them. The windows in some Moonie vans are tinted so unless you can see in from the front there is no way to know who is in what van. I was hoping to find out soon because both vans were pulling out of the gas station and they were going in two different directions. I had not seen Sandy get into either one of the vans, but I was hoping she was in one of these two. I decided to follow the same van she had been in all along. I had that plate number. The last place I wanted to start my day was to be directly right behind any Moonie van. That would be the wrong thing to do. They would surely figure out they were being followed. I had no choice, I had to fall in behind this van. The problem that occurred was as soon as their van had gone two blocks that is when the traffic stopped. Everyone was trying to get on to the road at the same time. Staying right in behind her was not an option. Just as traffic stopped, I turned into the road that the Moonie house was on. I had no choice; it was a quick decision. I pulled into the driveway of the house I had to walk around the night before. I was glad no one was up and moving around. I pulled out of the driveway and got back in line with the rest of the traffic. Lucky enough the time I spent in the neighbor's driveway was just enough time to pull up behind a farmer's wagon. Now I felt comfortable enough to pursue her van wherever it would take me. What I still did not know, was Sandy in this van? A couple hundred yards down the road the farmer's wagon turned into a field and now I was one car behind the van. I had not started freaking out yet. Just a few yards down the road was the last entrance to the field where the fair had taken place the night before. I was soon to find out that the van which was in front of me was filled with Moons security staff. Both vans stopped at the last entrance to the fair and blocked the traffic that was behind them. I was one of them. What surprised me next was crazy. The van in front opened its side door and out popped Sandy. At that same time, a large man that had been walking across the entrance hopped into Sandys van and Sandy jumped in behind him. Then they drove away. So why would a group of Moons solicitor's need a bodyguard? The large man that jumped into her van was nothing less than that. Why is he with them? Here we go again, I told myself, no more questions. It just does not make any sense. As soon as I could I called Sara and had her get my team together. I was not sure what was going to happen next, but I needed everyone ready. We had driven a few more miles and the security van that I was behind turned one way and Sandys van turned the other direction. I followed. Many hours passed by and we were still heading in the same direction. This is when it started to become clear to me. We were heading for New York City. There was no doubt in my mind. If it were not for the Moonies revival, we would have already been there. I would get the chance to call Sara back soon because we were ready for a gas stop. It did not take long before we were pulling into a big truck stop. I watched them pull up to the gas pumps and the big man got out and went into the store by himself. I pulled around to another pump and filled up. Shortly after that we were back on the road. I was able to reach Sara and have her send in my east coast team to New York City. It was a gamble, but I knew it was the right move. I was hoping I was right. We were not going to make it there tonight, so I was wishing for another Moonie house close by. We had been driving past dark and I was starting to wonder when they would catch on that they were being followed. It has been a long time since this whole adventure started and now, they had a well-trained security guy sitting in the middle seat of the van. He could have been watching out the back window and I would have never known it. This adventure needs to end soon, or my cover will be blown. One of the supplies I bought a while back were five-hour energy drinks. By now it is the only thing keeping me going. I have way too much time invested in this and I will not give up. Yes, I do talk to myself a lot. I am all I have for now. We had just taken a turn away from New York. Again, I was hoping for a Moonie house soon and close to a motel. The more we drove the more familiar I got with the area. I had been here before and yes there are a couple of Moonie houses close by. Sandy's crew just pulled off on an exit and I was close enough to see which direction they were heading. We should be arriving to their location soon. They turned onto the Moonies street, and I decided not to follow them. I was already pushing my luck. One of the things that I have learned about this cult is they are predictable when it comes to their schedule. They will rise and be ready to hit the road by seven am sharp. I decided to stay at a motel that I had stayed at before. It was located across the street from the store where the cult would buy their food. If they did not already have what they needed they will be by here in the morning. After a much-needed shower and a good rest I was back at their house and it was late. Their van was parked in the driveway and there were no lights on. I went back to my room. I needed to be back at their house by six am.

It was early the next morning and I had eaten breakfast and topped off my gas tank and was heading for their home. When I arrived, I parked up the road from their home and just like clockwork they had already loaded their van and were pulling out of the driveway. I followed. Here we go again. How long am I going to get away with this? Who knows? As we drove, we were not heading in the direction I was hoping for. I was starting to get tired of trying to figure out what they were going to do next even before they did it. I was not comfortable enough to just let them go and hope they would show up sooner or later were I thought they would. Too many things could go wrong, and I would always wonder if I had made that right decision. I was not ready to make that move, not yet. So, it was the same old thing, stay far enough behind them not to be seen, but not too far back and take the chance of losing them. Like I said, same old same old. We had not turned where we should have, and I just kept on following them. After driving for over one hour and being totally confused they were pulling into another Moonie house. Everybody went into the house and a few minutes later everyone plus one got into the van and they drove off. Like I said I am tired of trying to figure out what they are going to do next, so I just followed them. We had driven back the same way we came in to pick up this other person. Now we were heading in the right direction, finally. With any luck within the next five hours we should be pulling into another Moonie house in New York City. The next few hours seemed to drag on. No one to talk with but myself. What I would not have given back at the Moonie retreat for one of my security staff members. Well soon enough this part of this operation should be over. We had just gotten off the exit where we needed to be. I am happy to be back in this area, where I had spent a lot of time working with different cult groups. I knew my way around. Being in the outskirts of New York City and knowing the back roads will help. Within ten minutes we should be arriving at our location. Bingo, we have arrived.

Everyone that was getting out had already done so. The newcomers that were picked up and the driver drove off. It was my belief that they were heading to the other Moonie house across town. Sandy did arrive to her final location where I believed she would be returning every night after a ten to fourteen-hour day. My work was done for at least tonight. My crew should be arriving soon. And Sandy's parents live close by. Now all I need to do is get Sandy's routine down so we can do our thing. After all I have been through the rest of this work will be a lot easier. I took a shot and checked into a motel that we had used before, and low and behold, my crew did the same thing. Sara got everyone here on time and for that I am grateful. Just knowing that they are in shouting distance makes things exactly right.

After meeting with them, I called the Fergie's and let them know we were in town and so was Sandy. I asked them to be ready and they said they were. They were only minutes away. It is kind of funny that I had to chase after Sandy all over the country only for her to end up here. But I was glad. It was good to get with my old teammates again. After spending a few hours in the lounge, it was time to get some rest. Tomorrow was going to come around early. In the morning I switched cars with one of my teammates and along with one of the female deprogrammers we were sitting up the street from Sandy's new home, waiting for her to start her day. When we arrived the van that had dropped Sandy and her teammates off was sitting in the driveway along with two other vans. I had rested and had blown off some steam, so I was ready for anything. It was nice having someone to tag along. It is also convenient that she is a girl. It looks less suspicious when a guy and a girl are traveling together. I wish she would have been with me from the start. Sandy and her sidekicks are pulling out of their driveway. Here we go again. The nice thing about it we are not going far. We drove around for about fifteen minutes and then we came to a stop. Sandy and one of her sidekicks were being dropped off at a small college. In front of the college were some smaller shops. There are always young people coming in and out of these shops. I would not be surprised if she worked two shifts at this location. Her side kick is walking away from her and is heading to a different part of the buildings. This is quite unusual. He is just far away enough to not be a threat. I called the team back at the motel and gave them our location. I asked them to come right away. After that I placed a call to Sandy's parents and told them to drop everything and to get to our location ASAP. If there was going to be a chance to grab Sandy today, I wanted to take that opportunity. I am tired of chasing her and I want her removed from this cult. Everyone arrived sooner than I thought they could. After going over everything with my teammates we decided we had plenty of time to make this work. I was glad that my team brought me down a few levels. I needed that. Once I collected my thoughts, I informed the parents what we were getting ready to do. If any one of my teammates say it is a no go, then a no go it is. Like they said it was early and we had plenty of opportunity to pull this off. This place would give us plenty of opportunities to pick our spot and to do it safely.

So far Sandy has not shown much focus on what she should be doing. I believed she would be looking for a quiet place to chant for a little while. She needed to get focused on Moons orders. She was put into the recruiting part of the cult's plans and she needed to do her job to keep her cult leaders off her back if she were to find any kind of peace in her life. The cult is hard on its followers to do what they are told to do. Sandy is no different. If she does not produce enough new recruits, she will be told that she is not worthy enough and she needs to pray a lot more for Moons forgiveness. As the day goes on, I do not believe that Sandy's partner, who is not too far away from her, will be working his way back towards her. If they stay for the second shift, which is not uncommon, they will probably be working side by side. I have witnessed this before in a few cults. In the back of my mind I am thinking if we do not get her soon then we will have to deal with her partner. It could get messy. After watching Sandy go into just one store, it was obvious to all of us she was not going to keep this up very much longer. I walked across the street to have a chat with my crew. Before I could say a word, they picked up on what we were seeing, and they said let us do this. They had been there long enough to get comfortable with this area. They had already talked it over with each other and that was that.

One of my security staff informed me that the parents wanted to talk with me. I walked across the street where they were staying out of sight. They were getting nervous and I understood that. I assured them that they had the best team in the world working for them and they would get the job done. That made them a little happier. I told them that we were ready and as soon as Sandy showed her face, we would move in. I could tell they both were worried that something could go wrong and that was understandable. Sandy had been in the one shop for some time now and she should be coming out soon. I asked which one of the parents wanted to come with me and make the positive identification of their daughter. The father said he would. I walked with him around the corner so he could get a good look when Sandy came out of the store.

He started to sweat a little. The few minutes that it took Sandy to walk out the front door had to seem like forever for her father. The look on his face said everything. I told him to wait for our back up car to come and pick him up. One of my guys had already picked up the mother and he had her in the front seat ready to go. I took over his position while he got into his new position. When Sandy came out of the store she was not alone. She had made her first recruit for the day and she was standing outside of the store giving the young woman the direction to their house for dinner. What happened next changed a few things for us. The two of them started walking down the sidewalk in the same direction. We needed to see what was going to happen next before we could move in. As they were walking, they were talking. It did not seem like they were going to split up and that was going to create a small problem. If we could help it, we would like to do our thing with out to many witnesses. Either way everyone was in position and ready to move at a given notice. Shortly we would have the answer we were waiting for. When the two of them reached the next store, they split up. The new recruit went into the store and Sandy started walking towards the direction where her partner was working. She had to pass at least three more stores before she would be at the corner. There was an empty lot next to the corner and then the stores started up again. I made the decision to pull my car down to the corner. This is where the back of the shops were located. I knew my teammates picked right up on it. Sandy was either going to stop in one of the shops she was walking by or she was going to continue down the road to the end of the shops where she would find peace of mind to collect her thoughts before moving forward in doing Moons dirty work. I could tell that the short distance from her home to this area did not give her enough time to chant before she was dropped off and expected to jump right into things. I believe her teammate was a lot more seasoned than she was and he did not need the extra time. But she did. It was only a matter of seconds before she would reach where I was parked with her mother in the front seat. My teammates played it perfectly just like I knew they would. They were standing around the corner hidden from sight. If Sandy was going to head my direction, then she would walk right by my crew and never expect a thing. I told her mother to duck down in the seat. I did not want Sandy to see her mother right away. We always bring along one of the parents with us in the pickup car so she would not think that she was being molested or worse. Once she saw her mother's face, I knew things would go a lot smoother. All of this should only take about seven seconds, and that was all we needed to pull this off safely. Well it would not be long now. (I hope you are sitting there thinking about what it would be like to be one of my security staff members now). It is cool. When Sandy reached the corner, she would not walk any farther if she thought something was wrong. She is turning the corner and so far, she has not stopped.

She just walked past my two security guys and now she was just a few feet away from my car. I reached back and opened the back door and my two security guys helped Sandy into the back of my car. With one security guy sitting on each side of her, I told the mother to show herself. By this time, we were driving away, and no one was any wiser. Our back up had everyone else in his car and he was right behind me. When Sandy sat up in the back seat, she saw her mother and she started to cry. This was the first time I had ever seen anyone react like that. When Sandy started to cry so did her mother. It was beautiful. I just kept on driving as the two of them kept on crying.

Sandy's mother reached back and grabbed her arm and Sandy did nothing to stop her. This was a good sign. We have a forty five-minute drive to our safe house but first we must get out of the city. This was not going to be that easy. Even though I did know my way around it was not going to be a breeze doing so. The roads in New York City change daily. New construction appears out of nowhere. Construction barrels spring up everywhere. Roads close and reopen almost daily. Police officers are everywhere. Directing traffic, giving out tickets, chasing bank robbers, you name it. New York City has it all. One never knows when he is going to run into trouble. Add in the fact that we just kidnapped someone off the street, well you get the picture. Up to this point Sandy had been calm. But that could change at any time. Once it really soaks in what she just went through she may lash out. So far so good, and that makes me happy. Now all I had to do is get us out of the city in one piece. We are two blocks from reaching the traffic light that takes us out of New York City across the bridge. After that it is all highway to our safe house. But there was a problem. A police officer was directing traffic at the light. I could not afford to pull up beside him and wait for the light to change. Sandy had been quiet so far. If she sees the police officer, I do believe she is going to get loud. My crew was ready for that to happen. If she were going to cry out my team mates along with myself would start to sing as loud as we could, in hopes of drowning out her cries. The police in New York are used to seeing and hearing everything. I still was not going to put myself up next to him for any reason. I decided to creep along as slow as I could until the light turned green or when I would be motioned to move ahead. Either way I am going through the light no matter what color it turns to be. The last thing I want to do is turn right on red because that takes me back to where I had just come from. I was not going to go through all of that again only to end up in the same place. Either way we were creeping along at five miles an hour with no one in front of me and my back up car on my tail. The last thing I wanted to do was bring attention to myself, but I was looking stupid putting along at this speed. I had been in tough positions before, but this was a little different. I could see the entrance to the bridge in front of me. I was going to wing it like I have always done in the past and hope for the best. I looked up and saw the officer wave us through. We did what we usually do when coming out of a stressful situation, we yelled, hooped, and hollered as we drove past the policeman. It would not have mattered if Sandy would shout out, we sounded like a bunch of nuts driving over the bridge.

As a security team what makes us so special is, we are always on the same page. And for that I am grateful. We did what we had to do to make it work and If Sandy's mother had not been sitting in the front seat things would have turned out different. We have always needed the parents help and always will. Sandy's choice to not act out, showed the doubt she had in the cult, and that was a good thing. The final test is when we must go through the toll booth. This will give her another chance to cry out if she decides to. Again, we were ready. Sandy nor her mother was aware that our back up car drove around us a while back and he just went through the toll gate and paid for us. I did not have to stop. I kept looking back in the rear mirror to see if she was going to act out, but she did not. At that point I realized she had enough of this religious cult stuff, and she was looking for a way out. Understand she had been under mind control and that is not something you can just walk away from without the proper help. We were here to give her that help. We finally arrived at our safe house and she was being quiet. When we escorted her into the house, I asked her if she was tired and did, she want to take a nap and she said yes. I also asked her if she wanted her mom to sit with her while she went to sleep. She started to cry so I took that to be a yes. This was out of the norm for me to do this, normally the deprogrammers would start talking to her right off the bat. But this was not a normal case. The deprogrammers always had the last say in everything, but in this case they all agreed with me. That did make me feel a lot better. I never want to step on anyone's toes. This just seemed to be the right thing to do. Sandy would go on to sleep for fourteen hours and when she woke up her mother was sitting there holding her hand. I watched as Sandy smiled at her mother when she saw her sitting there. It was a wonderful sight. I asked her if she was ready for a shower and she smiled again. Her father had cooked breakfast for her, and it was waiting for her when she finished her shower. Everyone commented on how well rested she looked. Well this was different than any other case I had been on. No yelling, no fighting, and no arguments. I could really get used to this. It did not take long for her to be deprogrammed. Even so the deprogrammers took the time that was needed to reach her and to do whatever was necessary to help her in any way they could. We all enjoyed her company and after ten days with her it was time to take her and her parents to our rehab facility where, they would spend the next thirty days getting reunited again. Over the next thirty days Sandy had a lot of questions and the deprogramming staff was with her all the way to the end. Everyone is doing well and for me I decided this would be the last religious cult case I would take on. One of the hardest things I had to do, was to stop doing what I loved to do so much. But I had a family and family always must come first. Both of my girls were growing up to fast and I needed them in my life. Working against these cults is a full-time job, and it really takes a toll on our family lives. I will miss everyone and all the great kids I have come to know.

There is a lot I would like to say but cannot. It is hard trying to stay below the radar when it comes to staying one step ahead of the law. I learned a long time ago that we have never been ahead of law enforcement. They have always known of our whereabouts and they know exactly who we are. What we had done for so many years would not have been possible if it were not for law enforcement. From the local police to the state highway patrol and all the way up the ladder to the FBI. My special thanks go out to all of them. I wish I could say more but that would not be wise. I hope my readers have enjoyed the story's I have written. Not everyone can be a superhero or a private eye. We still need lawyers, policeman, and first responders. These people are the real heroes.

The next and last story I have written has nothing to do with religious cults or deprogrammings. It was the hardest story I had to write. It is a true story and I wish it were not. Writing about it had to be done. I hope it opens your eyes and touches your heart as it has touched mine.

CHAPTER SIXTEEN

FINAL STORY: JESSE

This last story is not about any Religious cults or Deprogrammings. This is the hardest case I have ever had to face. And that is saying a lot. Over my career I have gone through a lot. I have been hit, punched, smacked in the head, cut with broken glass, threatened, attacked, thrown to the ground, and I have even been propositioned, along with some other things I cannot say. Needless to say, in this line of work it puts us in some crazy places and around some not so nice people. These stories have never been about me. If I could change things, I do not believe I would change much, until this case came along. I am not concerned about myself but for the young adults that got lost in the cult system. For those who remain I wish I were a lot younger so I could continue to save each and every one of them. But that is impossible, and that is a word I have never wanted to use.

This takes me to my final story. It is a true story about a five-year-old little boy. I am going to call him Jesse. Jesse was the victim of abuse from his own mother and her boyfriend. I had been out of the spy business for some time now and I received a call from a family member. I was being asked to come out of retirement and take on this case. After listening to my family member talk about this little boy, I was heartbroken and angry. This was a case sent by God and I did not really understand myself until later in the case. I do not believe I could have turned it down even if I wanted to. Someone upstairs was not going to let me. I think some of you may agree after reading this story.

I was told by Jesse's grandmother that the local police and the FBI were brought in to search for Jesse because of his age. I was informed the FBI believed that Jesse had been taken out of Ohio and into Florida. To my understanding that is where they were conducting their search. I explained to Jesse's grandmother if the FBI and the police were on the case, what could I do that they could not? Why did she need my help? I was not sure what I would be able to do. I am just one person and they are many. But I knew it was just an excuse on my part. I did not believe it for a minute. Someone or thing was behind me pushing me mentally to go forward. If Jesse was still on this planet, I was going to find him and remove him from these two-evil people. I had never been so driven in my life and I was going to take advantage of it. My drive was being fueled by a higher power. I did believe my background may come in handy, but this case was different. All I knew was I had to try. I called the grandmother and told her I would do everything I could, and she was pleased. The grandmother had gotten custody of Jesse after photos of abuse were shown to a judge by a case worker, but up to now no one was able to find him. I had been in a different line of work when she requested my help. I decided to take some time off and start my search.

I gathered up as much information as I could on the mother, her boyfriend and their families and friends. There was little known information on what had been done or was going on in the search for Jesse. Or at least law enforcement was not saying. This is what I was able to find out. The mother was on welfare and she had been receiving food stamps. That was not going to do me any good. The FBI would be all over that. The boyfriend was a total sleaze bag. He could not keep a job and now he was being investigated on child abuse. The mother had no car, and her boyfriend's car puffed smoke, and when it was shut off it had to be jumped to get it started .The police didn't know what kind of car he drove or if it even had a license plate on it. It did not seem like very much information to go on, but it was all I needed. I did what I always did when I wanted to clear my head, I took a drive in the country. I found no distractions and a sense of peace.

After driving around for a while, I parked my car in a park and started writing down everything I thought I knew. The way I understood it to be, both the mother and her boyfriend were broke. The car they were driving was a piece of junk. All their family members and their friends lived in Ohio. I concluded that these two people had burned a lot of bridges. I did not agree with the FBI's thinking, that they were somewhere in Florida. The boyfriend was an exceptionally large man who had many belts in the martial arts. And it was my understanding from the grandmother, anyone that knew the boyfriend feared him. She said he was a badass with a short temper. The more I learned about these two buttheads the angrier I became. I just knew they were still in Ohio and they were not far away. It was not a hunch; I just knew they were close. To my understanding neither one of them knew that the grandmother had gotten custody of Jesse. As far as I knew they did not even know they were being hunted by the FBI. One of the things that I honestly believed was the mother knew she had done wrong in harming her child. And I also believed she was afraid of her boyfriend. These are some of the reasons why they were keeping a low profile. They were not going to leave the state in the car they were driving. Besides everyone they knew lived here. They had no one else to sponge off of. His martial arts teacher was here in Ohio. Someone was hiding them but who? I drove around this area for a couple days. Why this area I was not sure. When I looked back on it, I really had no idea why I chose this area to start with. Usually I would have had an idea but not this time. This was not like me. What was going on with me, I could not put my finger on it. This area was country with a lot of farms, not a lot out here. Not much at all.

I decided to get my old boss involved. You remember him I called him C. I called C and told him what I was doing. I asked him if he had the time to pull a few strings for me. I needed someone to do some leg work for me and he always knew how to open doors when no one else could. I could be searching for Jesse for a while and I needed some other things done. He was the right person for the job. For some reason I just could not stop thinking that if these two buttheads get wind that they are being hunted they would try to go deeper into hiding. C suggested that we get a conservatorship to use when we needed it. I was aware of what it was, but I had never had the opportunity to use one before. It would become the anchor for our case later on. Thanks, Mr. C. What a conservatorship does, at least in this case, is to give us access to whatever branch of law enforcement we deemed necessary to use them in retrieving this young boy. This was big. Now all I had to do was find Jesse and law enforcement would do the rest. It was a load off my mind. I had not figured out yet what I would do when I had to confront the mother's boyfriend. It is no longer an issue. I started devoting all my time in finding Jesse. It did not take me very long.

I had been driving around for a few days in the country and going over and over the same area with no luck. I knew better than to do this. There just was not anything out there but farms. I knew neither one of the buttheads were farmers. It was getting late, so I decided to grab my wife and daughter and drive around in the country some more. Do not ask me why I came back to this same location, but I did. We had just turned onto the same country road I had been driving on several times. When I drove up to the same four-way stop sign I had been at a hundred times, I smelled smoke. It was strong. There were a lot of farm tractors in this area, and it could have been one of them. But was it? I was not sure which way to turn. And to this day I still do not know why I chose the direction I did. Like I said it was a four way stop. I had three choices. I turned left and drove down the road a couple miles with my windows down. The smell was getting stronger. This time there was smoke to go with it. I caught up to what was making the smoke expecting to see a farm tractor, but much to my surprise it was just who I was looking for. In the back seat without a child restraint on was what looked like a little boy. In the front seat was both buttheads. I was hoping they were going home, but that would have been too easy. They drove for about five minutes and they pulled into a parking lot of a little country store. He shut off his car and they all went into the store. I was thinking they were going to be in there for some time or he would have left his car running. We were in a very small town and at that time it was not that unusual for people to leave their cars running when they were just picking up a few things. It was done all the time. My wife said my little girl had to use the bathroom. We only lived five minutes down the road, so I sent them home with the car. It should not take them long to get there and back. With his car sitting there not running and no other customers in the parking lot, he was going to have to wait to get a jump when he came out of the store. I figured we had time. I needed to get a better look at Jesse to make sure it was him. The only way to do that was to go into the store. The store they were in was a small country store. Even though the store was small it carried just about everything a person would need. It did not have many rows. I figured once I entered the store, I was going to be in a position I would have to walk past them to get a good look. As I walked past the small child what I saw was sickening. He had a broken arm with a cast on it. He had burns on the other arm and he had a black eye. I almost threw up. Something stopped me from doing so. It was not me that had control of my guts at that time. But for some reason the urge to throw up just went away. I could not explain it.

When I got up next to the mother and her boyfriend, I looked up on the shelf and eyed a big can of beans. All I could think about was grabbing that can on the shelf and hitting her boyfriend as hard as I could in the back of his head for what he had done to this small child. At that very moment I felt no fear of her boyfriend at all. Even though I knew what he was capable of. I could have brought him to his knees with no problem. Boy my adrenaline was flowing. I tried to tell myself why I did not crush his skull for what he had done. I kept telling myself it would have been the wrong thing to do but I did not believe it for a minute. There was only one thing that stopped me, and it was not me. I have never been any good at holding back my emotions especially when it comes to small children. To this day, I still can remember the strength I felt at that very moment. I have thought about that day many times and I honestly believe I did not have control of my actions. My thoughts did not coincide with my actions and that is just not me. It was hard for me to swallow. After making a positive identification I walked out of the store to the phone booth next door. I called C and he answered. He was at the Cleveland police department giving surveillance classes to their staff. I explained to C I had found Jesse and the kind of shape he was in. I needed the conservatorship paperwork right away. He told me he had it in his briefcase, and he was leaving right away to bring it to me. He was over fifty miles away. It was going to take time even with the police lights and sirens blasting. I was praying he would make it in time. A lot could happen in that amount of time. I would have given a lot of money to have that small piece of paper in my hand. The

Cleveland police department contacted the local police department in my area and had them dispatch a cruiser to my location. Shortly after I hung up with C the local police pulled in. The officer arrived alone, and he was not sure why he was there. He was told there was a domestic abuse case and to get here as soon as possible. I explained to him I had a conservatorship on its way to him and he was to hold the people that owned that car. I went on to explain what was going on and I could not blow my cover at this time until the owner of that car was taken into custody. I explained to him they would be coming out of the store at any time. I walked across the parking lot and stood were I could not be seen. They finally walked out of the store with their groceries and put them into his car. What happened next should not have happened, but it did. The police officer pulled his car over to the buttheads car and gave them a jump. I could not believe what I was watching. There was nothing I could do. It was hard watching the buttheads pulling out of the parking lot one way and the officer driving out the other way. Now I was wishing that I had hit him in the head with that can of beans. That little boy's life was in danger and that is all I can think about. I wanted to run after them on foot and if I would have been in a little better shape I would have done so. I was stuck with no car and the local police had just let that monster loose. A few minutes later my wife drove back into the parking lot. I ran over and jumped into the driver's seat and started my pursuit once again. They were too far ahead of me by now, but I could still smell the oil burning from their car. I came up to another four way stop sign, and I did not know which way to go. I did not have time to go the wrong way. Then I remembered my old days when I drove a car that also burned oil. One thing about oil burning cars is that they also leak oil as well. I got out of the car and looked down at the road. It was apparent which way they went. There were oil drippings on the road, and they were fresh. I turned that direction and a few blocks down the road there was an old farmhouse on the left-hand side. Their car was backed into the driveway. All the car doors were open, and it looked like they had left their groceries in the car. Standing in the front yard stood three of buttheads martial art buddies. It was my belief they were spooked, and they had no intentions on staying in this area. They were inside packing to leave. His buddies were here to make sure his departure went smoothly. I was hoping it would take these guys longer to get packed than it will take me to get back to the little store where C should be arriving. I turned around as fast as I could and made my way back to the little store. When I arrived, C was waiting for me. He was with the chief of police from Cleveland Police department, and of course my conservatorship. Parked beside them was a state policeman. He was holding the conservatorship in his hand. He had heard the conversation from the local policeman that jumped the buttheads car. Things did not sound right to him, so he decided to come by and lend a hand. I told everyone there was not any time to get caught up to date because if I were right, they would be pulling out of their driveway anytime now. The state highway patrol officer said ok lead the way. I got into my car with my wife and my oldest child and pulled out onto the road and I never looked back. I was not worried about the speed limit or stopping at any stop signs. All

I knew was I had two police cars on my ass. I stopped short of the farmhouse because I still had my family with me. I pointed the house out to the state highway patrolman. Thank goodness their car was still sitting in the driveway. When the state highway patrolman got out of his car my jaw dropped. He was close to seven feet tall and he was larger than life itself. He said he would take it from here. I was not sure what that meant but I was about to find out, we all were. He pulled his car into their driveway and got out of his car walked right by buttheads martial arts buddies that were standing by the front door. They moved out of his way without saying a word. He walked up the steps and knocked on the door. I could not hear if he was invited in or not, but a few seconds later he was on the other side of the front door. He had gone in by himself. We all sat and waited to see what was going to happen next. Within five minutes the front door opened and what happened next touched my heart. He walked out the front door with Jesse in his arms. He walked over to his car and took out a car seat from the trunk of his car and he strapped Jesse into the back seat of his car. I turned to C and the captain and asked what was going to happen to Jesse next. I was told he was on his way to the hospital where he would spend some time there healing. Tears finally started forming on my face. Whoever was directing me to this happy ending had let the flood gates open and it felt good. I have not won all the battles that I had to fight. But this one I knew from the start that the ending would be won by the good guys. How did I know when and where to start my search? How did I know which way to make my turns to find Jesse? What kept me from hitting the boyfriend in the head?

What made me find Jesse when the FBI did not? And how could I find Jesse in such a short time? I cannot explain all that has come about. What I do know was I was able to do something out of the ordinary and I did not do it alone. I want to give a special thanks to the grandmother that is no longer with us. The officers that played such a big part of bringing this home. To C and his wonderful wife that gave me my start. And to my family for understanding how important my work was to me and putting up with all the times I was not home.

As for Jesse he was in good hands. As far as the two buttheads, it is sad to say they were not severely punished, although they had to pay the piper. In my thoughts they both should have gotten the same thing they put Jesse through. I still wish that I would have picked up that can of beans.

I hope you enjoyed reading my stories as much as I did writing them.

THE END

CPSIA information can be obtained
at www.ICGtesting.com
Printed in the USA
LVHW051620100720
660328LV00007B/682

9 781641 118613